A 9-PART
LIFE-SAVING
SYSTEM!

NEW PREPPER'S SURVIVAL BIBLE

CARLOS MACK

THE ULTIMATE LONG-TERM
SURVIVAL HANDBOOK
FOR PROTECTING YOUR
FAMILY & BEING PREPARED
WHEN DISASTER STRIKES

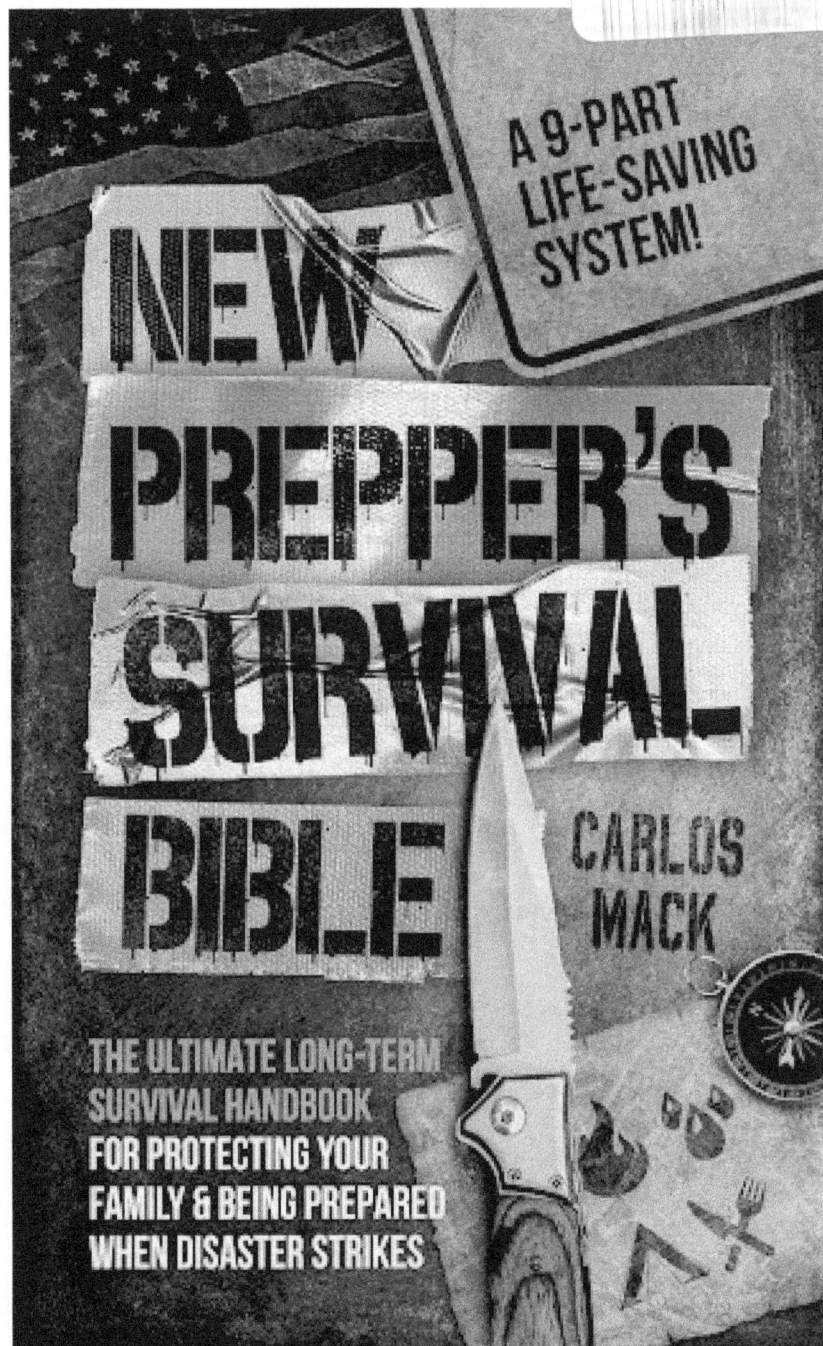

New Prepper's Survival Bible

The Ultimate Long-term Survival Handbook for Protecting Your Family & Being Prepared When Disaster Strikes

Carlos Mack

http://www.lighthousesurvival.net

Contents

System #3 - IDEA: Identify, Develop, Execute, Analyze
The Life-saving Acronym for Long-term Survival

System #4 - KISS: Keep It Simple, Stupid
Building Your Prepper's Pantry

System #5 - WIG: Water, Industrial Bulk Food, Gear
Stockpiling Guide for Practical Home Storage Items

System #6 - GROW: Goals, Research, Options, Work
GARDEN Off-Grid to Feed Your Family

System #7 - HOME: Heat, Outsmart, Munitions, Educate
Shelter in Place and Defend Your Disaster-Ready Turf

System #8 - MASH: Medical, Accessories, Self-Defense, Hygiene
You never know when and where an emergency will happen

System #9 - STOP: Stop, Think, Observe, Plan
Bugging Out for Survival

HOW TO GET $49 WORTH OF PREPPER'S CONTENT

FREE

- Free bonus #1: Food Storage Family Inventory Calculator Spreadsheet   ($19 value)

- Free bonus #2: Walmart Shopping List ($12 value)

- Free bonus #3: Recipes Made From Your Prepper Pantry ($10 value)

- Free bonus #4: Bug Home Guide ($8 value)

JUST FOR YOU!

As a way of saying THANK YOU for your purchase, I'm offering you these 4 FREE bonus gifts exclusive to my readers!

To receive your bonuses scan the QR code below:

SCAN ME

Introduction - When Rome Falls

I want you to think about someone who matters to you - your husband or wife, or perhaps one of your kids or your neighbor. Picture them in your mind. What do they look like? What little things do they do that make you love them? Are they sweet? Silly? I want you to focus on that for a moment and really, truly cling to that image, memorizing everything about it. Think about how you'd describe them to me.

Now, imagine that the only thing between them and death is how well you've planned for the unexpected.

I know some of you are smirking and thinking that this is corny. It absolutely is corny - until it happens to you. Countless people who once smirked have learned the hard way that just because things are good right now, it does not mean times will always be good. Natural disasters happen. Economic turmoil and rioting happen. Man-made disasters, wars, looting, supply chain problems, you name it - *they all happen.* I think that COVID shook a lot of people up because it showed that the system can't always be trusted and, every now and then, things go very wrong in a way you never saw coming. Even capable, educated people have been caught totally off guard when life throws them a curveball.

When these things happen and lives hang in the balance, any amount of preparation in the here and now will help. You don't want to be that person in the snowstorm fighting through the ice trying to find food when all the power goes out. You don't want to be that person who's coming up with a plan *after* a disaster hits.

You want to be the person who's ready *now,* and if that disaster ever strikes, you'll be able to rest easy knowing that you've taken the steps necessary to ensure your family's survival. What this looks like depends entirely on the specific disaster and your family's needs.

This brings me to the most important question: **Who is this book for?**

It's for the suburban dad who was not prepared during COVID and wants to be better prepared for the next thing that comes along. It's for the closet prepper who's been quietly gathering supplies over the past 5 or 10 years but is afraid to tell their neighbors and friends. It's for the survival expert who's ready for a full-blown apocalypse. It's for *you*. Right now, *you*. Whatever your education, location, or financial or family situation, you have the ability to rest easy knowing that you've done what you need to do, so that in the next situation, you won't be the one left behind. All you have to do is start taking the right steps now.

Let's move to the second most important question: **Why will this book help you?**

It's a vital question. Why buy this book? Why care? What are you actually going to get out of this? Here's how I'd explain it: Each one of you is in your own stage of preparing for disasters. Some of you have arsenals, and some of you just buy extra toilet paper so you don't run out if the store runs out. The way that I've designed this book is to provide ways for you to be better prepared, step-by-step, no matter if you're a total novice or a seasoned expert. At first, we'll cover some of the basics, such as why you should prep and what food you should keep in your pantry, and then we'll move toward more advanced stuff, like bugging out and what to put in your first-aid kit.

Prepping shouldn't be complicated or stressful. It should be something that puts you more at ease, and it doesn't need to cost a fortune. This is a collection of actionable, understandable steps for you to take and the reasons behind them.

Each step of the way, I'll be here to walk you through it. Everything I say is backed with thorough research and 15 years of prepping experience. Not only do I personally practice the principles covered in this book with my own family, I am constantly learning and studying the craft to improve my skills and ability to stay alive if a catastrophic event should occur.

My hope is that you'll use this prepper bible as a reference guide to look up items of interest along your journey; however, I strongly recommend that you read the entire thing cover to cover first. It does not have Old and New Testaments like the Good Book it's named after, but the table of contents should clearly direct you to the systems related to whatever topic you may want to dig deeper into.

Reading this book doesn't make you a paranoid person. It doesn't put a stigma on you like the word "prepper" used to. Today it means that you're a person who's ready for the next big one. Throughout history, humans have been programmed for survival. It's the reason we're the most dominant species on earth. In the past, survival techniques were necessary for everyday life - you either successfully kill the bear or it eats you. You either know how to treat that wound or it gets infected. You either know how to forage or you starve.

Life isn't like that anymore. Many of us have comfortable, cushy lives, and very rarely do we have to wonder how we will survive if it was all just gone, even if only for a few days. How many of us are actually prepared for a worst-case scenario? People were mostly quite happy and trusting of the system, and then COVID hit. The COVID-19 pandemic pulled back the curtain to show the world how dangerous total faith in the free market can become. Even Rome, the most sophisticated and advanced society in the ancient world, eventually collapsed.

Are our resources unlimited? Does our government always provide? Do they even tell us the truth? It seems like, recently, man-made and natural disasters are around every corner. People are angrier and more closed off than ever. Lots of people have stopped watching the news entirely to avoid that creeping anxiety that comes with it.

After what we've been through with COVID, and looking back on countless examples of unexpected disasters, I think the answer is clear: We need to be better prepared. You need to store extra food and water for an emergency. You should reevaluate your home in terms of how disaster-ready it truly is in today's world. This may sting, but, if you're willing, you can even look in the mirror and do an honest assessment with yourself regarding how positive and resourceful your mindset is for emergency preparedness. We all can improve and grow, and this book teaches sustainability in a disposable world. Besides, there is no knight in shining armor coming over the hill to rescue you. In a worst-case scenario event, *you* are the backup!

It's okay if you're a beginner in the prepping world. Through my life experiences, thorough research, and passion for everything related to emergency preparedness, this book has broken down the best prepping knowledge in easy-to-follow strategies and advice. Of course, this takes having an open mind, a positive attitude, and a healthy appetite for learning. I'm going to walk you through everything step-by-step until you've mastered the skills necessary for you and your family to *thrive* through the next catastrophic event.

Ready?

System #1 - The 5 W's: Who, What, When, Where, and Why?

Are YOU Prepared?

"There are risks and costs to action. But they are far less than the long-range risks of comfortable inaction."

— John F. Kennedy

Everyone has to start somewhere. For people like you and me, that somewhere was probably when we realized that we couldn't depend on the government or the supply chain to meet our needs. Whether that happened during the COVID pandemic, in the shortages that have followed it, or in a natural disaster that struck our hometown, we came to that realization. The question is… Now what?

The good news is that we humans are hard-wired for survival. It may not seem like it, but we are. We've just allowed society to cover those more basic instincts with a whole lot of comfort. Brush off that layer of comfort and those instincts can surface. Then it's just a matter of what to do with them.

If you're reading this book, it means that those survival instincts have been awakened in you. You're concerned about what might happen when the next disaster comes along. You've seen how the government has failed and how difficult it became to buy even the most basic things. Even more importantly than that, you've come to realize that you're going to have to do something to make sure that your family is taken care of the next time a problem comes along.

This is the ideal time for that realization, because there are more resources available to those who want to prepare than ever before. A generation ago, people who wanted to prepare had to make do with camping gear that wasn't built for their needs and food from the grocery store. Today, there are a myriad of products developed just for survival.

We're going to look at what it takes to survive and what you can do to ensure your family's survival. By the time we reach the end of this book, you'll have gained many key skills for emergency preparedness. But it all starts with you and who you are.

Chapter 1
WHO are Preppers?

Preppers are both ordinary people and some of the most extraordinary people you'll ever meet. They're ordinary in that you can find preppers in all walks of life. Your kid's teacher, the guy you sit next to at work, a neighbor, or even your pastor at church could be a prepper and you'd never know it. Most preppers live pretty ordinary lives, keeping their prepping activities under wraps. What makes people preppers, more than anything, is a decision to take responsibility for their own lives. Rather than depending on "Big Brother" to take care of them and their family, they've decided that they will do what it takes to make sure that they're prepared.

If there's anything that the COVID pandemic and other recent disasters have shown us, it's that none of us know what's coming next. Preppers simply decide that, regardless of what that next thing is, they're going to be ready for it. So they learn skills, stockpile supplies, buy survival gear, and generally build their lives around the idea that they might have to survive without all the comforts, the infrastructure, and the supplies they're used to.

If you think about it, this is how our ancestors lived all through history. Those who lived in colder climates had to prepare for winter, stocking food to get them through to the next year. Those in warmer climates didn't have to worry about winter so much, but they did have to be concerned about hurricanes and other disasters. There was no FEMA to bail anyone out, so they made sure that they were ready to bail themselves out.

Unlike what we've seen in the popular show *Doomsday Preppers*, the average prepper isn't preparing for one catastrophic event that they are convinced is coming. Real preppers, as opposed to the Hollywood kind, prepare for any and all disasters. They recognize that "the big one" can come, but they're mostly concerned about whatever kind of natural disaster their region of the country is likely to encounter. Prepping for one thing is essentially preparing for everything.

It's really hard to say just how many preppers there are out there. Before COVID, most preppers and prepping websites would have put that number at about 2% of the population. But the pandemic changed all that. The great toilet paper shortage of 2020 was an eye opener to a lot of people, showing us all just how fragile our supply chain is. This caused many more people to join the ranks of the preppers, even if they only did that on a short-term basis. Now that COVID is behind us, some of those people will move on, leaving the prepping life behind; others are hooked and are becoming true preppers as they prepare for the future.

One of the things that has hurt the prepping movement is what television and the media have made of it. According to *Doomsday Preppers*, all preppers are paranoid maniacs who buy into every conspiracy theory that comes along and are convinced that the world is about to end by some specific catastrophe. Nothing could be further from the truth. By and large, preppers are some of the most level-headed people around. Yes, there are a few nutcases around, but, as with any other part of society, they are the exceptions.

Preppers don't all live underground in bunkers made from shipping containers. (Actually, shipping containers make very poor bunkers, as they aren't strong enough to support the dirt that's put over them.) Yes, there are a few preppers who have bunkers, and even a few who have somehow made them out of shipping containers, but that isn't common.

Nor are all preppers wealthy. The prepping movement has reached the nouveau riche in Silicon Valley, where tech business owners buy islands or properties in New Zealand to bug out to. But that isn't the average prepper. Most are middle class people who live a financially conservative lifestyle and spend money on prepping instead of buying toys of one sort or another.

Preppers are extraordinary as well in that they have skills and knowledge that most people don't have today. They're the ones who are ready to deal with the next disaster and have the supplies to make it through.

Chapter 2
WHAT is Prepping?

The concept of prepping is an old one, although the term itself is rather new. If we go back in time, our ancestors had to learn how to deal with storms, drought, and winter freezes. While the disasters they faced were different across the world, depending on climate, terrain, and the like, every place had its challenges. The people living there had to learn how to preserve and stockpile food, cut firewood to get through the winter, and dig wells so that they would have water to drink. Pretty much everything we do in prepping today our ancestors did years ago, simply so they could survive.

Your own grandparents and great-grandparents were probably preppers, although they didn't call themselves by that name. They didn't have the massive infrastructure and supply chains that we have available to us today. Many of them grew their own food, and the majority of the products they bought were manufactured locally, often by artisans, who were specialists in working with that type of material. A "furniture factory," for example, would be a local cabinet-making shop, employing several carpenters who knew how to make a variety of different types of furniture.

The colonization period and westward expansion couldn't have happened if people were dependent on a supply chain. Much of it was fueled by homesteaders, who would go out and stake claims on land, building their own home, plowing the land, and bringing in a harvest. They mostly ate what they grew in their vegetable garden, selling their excess produce to buy the few store-bought items that they had to have.

To survive such a lifestyle, people had to be able to do a wide variety of tasks that are not part of life today. It started with choosing a plot of land to homestead, which would give them the basic resources they needed. Growing their own food was a necessity, so they had to have adequate rain. But they also needed water for the home, which meant drawing water from the creek, spring, or well. Every winter, they would cut firewood for the next year, so their homestead had to be near the woods to provide a source for that firewood.

This was the norm for much of human history. As towns and cities grew, people were able to focus more and more on their specialty, paying others to produce goods they needed. But those luxuries only existed in the cities; the farther out a family lived, the more they had to depend on themselves. While that made for a hard life, it also made for hearty people who were more likely to survive life's hardships.

Prepping vs. Survivalism

Before the modern prepping movement came along, people who prepared for disasters were called "survivalists." Today, many people see the two terms as synonymous. But while there is a considerable amount of crossover between the two, there is actually quite a bit of difference.

The easiest way to remember the difference is that prepping is a lifeline, while survivalism is a lifestyle. Many people prepare, building stockpiles of equipment and supplies, so that they are ready to survive whatever disaster comes their way - but that doesn't necessarily make it a lifestyle. On the other hand, a true survivalist is more focused on gaining knowledge so that they can survive without the food stockpile. While they might actually have food and other supplies stored up, they are not as dependent on them. Rather, they can survive by hunting, fishing, and gathering edible plants.

As the prepping movement has grown, so has the focus. Most people start out as preppers, building a stockpile of supplies. Those who stick with it start learning survival skills, eventually reaching the point where they are more survivalist than prepper. This makes the prepping and survival community a true mix of people who are part prepper and part survivalist.

Chapter 3
WHEN Should You Prepare?

Prepping is not a one-time activity, nor should it be something you only plan for once, simply to forget it when that disaster does not happen. True prepping is something that needs to be happening a little bit at a time, all the time.

Few of us can afford to just run out and buy an extra month's worth of food in one trip over and above our regular grocery bill, let alone several months' worth. But you can get organized now by making a list of prepping items and shopping during those times when you have a few extra dollars left over in your monthly budget.

Common Events for Emergency Preparedness

There are many different disasters we might prepare for, but they can all be broken down into three basic categories:

- **Personal Disasters** – This includes the loss of a job, loss of a family member, or a sickness which makes it impossible to work. These are mostly financial disasters that strike only your family. Even so, they can be difficult to survive.
- **Regional Disasters** – Stepping it up from there, we can find situations where our whole town or state is affected by the disaster. The Camp Fire that burned down Paradise, California, fits in this category, as well as any hurricane or major blizzard. Not only is your family affected by the disaster, but so is everyone nearby who might be able to help. Any help that comes will have to come from outside the region.
- **Major Disasters** – This category of disasters covers things that affect an entire nation, such as the COVID-19 pandemic, the Ukraine War, or an EMP attack on our country. They are often referred to as TEOTWAWKI events (The End of the World as We Know It) because the way we live our lives is forced to change. Who would have ever thought that we'd need to social distance or wear masks everywhere we went before the COVID pandemic? Other major

disasters, like the loss of the electrical grid, could be even worse.

If we look back over the last few decades, we can see a trail of constant major disasters which have either plagued or threatened our way of life. This often happens under most people's radar, as people tend to ignore any potential for worst-case scenarios. Nevertheless, any of these could have changed life as we know it in as little as a day.

- **The Cold War** – Our younger generation didn't grow up during this, but for over 40 years the world lived under the constant threat of thermonuclear war. Had it become a hot war, it could have killed over half the world's population, including those who would have died from starvation.
- **Y2K** – There was a real scare that all of our computers would crash when the clock turned over from 1999 to 2000. Those computers had all been built with an internal calendar that ended at midnight on December 31, 1999. Nobody knew for sure how or if they would work when that time ran out, and they couldn't build computers fast enough to replace them all.
- **9/11** – The attack on the World Trade Center in New York City was the most catastrophic terrorist incident to ever hit our country. Islamic terrorists flew jumbo jets into the World Trade Center and the

Pentagon, destroying our national confidence, as well as causing a host of other problems.

- **Hurricane Katrina** – The most destructive natural disaster to strike our country to date, Hurricane Katrina was a Category 5 hurricane that hit the Gulf Coast, bursting the dykes that protected New Orleans, and flooding it.
- **The Great Recession** – A man-made incident, the housing crash of 2008-2009 led to millions of people losing their homes and, ultimately, the Great Recession.
- **COVID-19** – Totally unexpected, a previously unknown virus strain originating in China infected people all over the world and killed over 6 million people. During the early days of this pandemic, medical science had no idea how to treat it because they had not encountered it before.

People ask if preppers are sane or not. Looking over that list, I'd have to say that preppers are the sanest people amongst us. They are the only part of society that recognizes these great risks we live under, preparing to survive through whatever comes our way.

How Long to Prepare For?

One of the most challenging questions that preppers face is just how long to prepare for or how big a stockpile of supplies to build. There is no perfect answer for that, as none of us know just what disaster is coming our way, or how long it will last.

If you look at the information provided by various agencies, you will see that FEMA's "Ready.gov" website says to stock enough food and water for 3 days and the Red Cross says to have 14 days' worth of supplies. But when you compare that to real-life disasters, it may not be enough. There were people without running water and grocery stores without food up to 6 weeks after Hurricane Katrina hit New Orleans.

Most preppers just start stockpiling, adding to their stockpile as they go. The real problem isn't the disaster itself, but the recovery time after a disaster, which is usually much longer than the disaster itself. While emergency crews work to bring in relief supplies as quickly as they can, those resources are always stretched to the maximum. If you can get by without them, not only will it be safer for you, but it will leave more for others.

Think of the worst possible disaster that you can expect to strike where you live. How long will it take for the infrastructure and supply chains to be restored after that? Looking back on Hurricane Katrina, that was weeks longer than expected! So, once you figure out a number, double it - that's how long you should be prepared for.

Over and above that, there's the risk of true TEOTWAWKI events. The big one that people talk about is an attack by

EMP (electromagnetic pulse), where a nuclear device is exploded above the atmosphere, releasing enormous amounts of electrons which would destroy our electrical grid. That's not likely to be a recoverable disaster. According to the report of the EMP Commission, somewhere between 60 to 90% of our population would die, mostly from starvation. Prepping for that means being prepared to survive for years, mostly through growing our own food.

Chapter 4
WHERE to Prepare?

For most of us, the best place to prepare to survive a disaster is in our home. However, most of us live a lifestyle where we're away from home more often than not. Between work, school activities, and the organizations we belong to, it's rare to see the whole family at home at the same time.

This means that we need to be prepared no matter where we are. While our bug-in shelter is our home, we need to have a plan and the capability to work our way back home should a disaster hit. This means being ready to walk home if the roads are impassable or the car won't run. We'll need good walking shoes, a hat, and coat, as well as a basic survival kit.

Everyday Carry (EDC)

Preparedness starts at the most basic level with the things that we carry with us every day. Even this can be divided into two categories, as there are the things that we carry on our bodies, as well as those that we carry in an everyday carry bag - a "kit" of basic survival gear. While these can vary considerably from person to person depending on where you live and what you're likely to encounter, all have some things in common.

As far as what you carry on your person, that should include sufficient equipment to ensure you can meet the most basic survival needs if you're left without anything else:

- Weapon - to protect yourself, preferably a pistol if you can carry it legally
- Firestarter
- Tactical flashlight
- Pocket knife
- Spare cash
- Whistle - to call for help
- Identification
- Cell phone
- Laminated list of emergency phone numbers - in case your phone goes out

The next level should be an everyday carry bag (EDC bag), which can also be known as a get-home bag (GHB). This is essentially an urban survival kit, containing everything you need to have in order to survive a couple of days:

- Another firestarter - something both waterproof and easy to use
- Fire accelerant - something to get the fire burning if the fuel is wet
- Spare batteries for the flashlight
- Lightweight tarp for making a shelter
- Paracord and duct tape to use with the tarp
- Emergency blanket - reflects heat back to your body
- Rain poncho
- Water filter
- Water bottle
- Some high-energy food bars
- Collapsible cup
- Straight-bladed knife
- Knife sharpener
- Emergency phone charger - either solar or battery pack
- Small first-aid kit - equivalent of a military individual first-aid kit (IFAK)

This is actually a very minimal EDC or GHB bag. There are a lot of different ideas about what can and should be included in this bag. These items are nothing more than a starting point - as you learn more, you'll find more things to add to your own EDC bag.

Keep This in Your Desk or Locker

We're using the term "bugging in" for survival at home, but what if your bug-in ends up being at work? Ideally you want to get home, but you may find yourself in a shelter-in-place situation due to a gas line leak or a chemical spill. In that case, they're not going to let you go home, and you're going to have to make the best of it at work, perhaps even overnight.

Such emergencies can and do happen. While not as long-term as the results of even a regional disaster, we should be ready for them. I was at work a couple of years ago when a gas line exploded a mile from my location. The local government immediately called a shelter-in-place order for everyone within a 5-mile radius. I had to stay inside, waiting for the all-clear.

In addition to the everyday carry bag, there are a few things that are useful to keep in your desk or locker, ensuring that you'll have them in case of an emergency. These are things you might use in the office on a normal basis, which can also help you survive:

- **1-liter water bottle** – These have almost become a fad, but they can ensure that you have water if the water goes out. If you end up trekking your way home, the water bottle will also be useful.

- **Phone charger** – Always keep your phone charged as much as possible. Plugging it in at work or setting it on a charging pad will make sure that it's ready if an emergency occurs. You don't want to try to get home with only a 15% charge.

- **Laptop bag or backpack** – Carrying a laptop back and forth to work gives you a perfect way of hiding your EDC bag in plain sight. While you might not be able to fit everything you want inside, you can keep the most critical items in that bag and store the rest in your car. Hang a hand sanitizer on the outside and make sure to have a pen or pencil with waterproof paper. Some extra batteries for your flashlight would be useful as well.

- **Food** – Several of my coworkers, myself included, keep snacks in their desk drawers to help them get through the day. These should be nutritious snacks, like nuts, granola bars, and dried fruit. These types of snacks will keep you going a whole lot longer than chips and candy bars. Should you need to leave work and go home, you can grab them and put them in your pack.

- **Multi-tool** – The multi-tool has replaced the pocketknife for many people, combining a folding knife with a whole toolbox. It can be amazingly useful around the office, while also helping you make your way home.

Things to Put in Your Car Now

While your EDC bag will do a lot to take care of you and help you get home, it won't provide all your needs. One example is clothing - are the work clothes you're wearing appropriate for a 20-mile walk home? The sport coat or fleece jacket that you wear to the office won't be enough to keep you warm while trudging through the snow. Along the same lines, what woman is going to be able to walk a considerable distance in high heels?

Our next layer of preparedness is what to put in your car:

- **Clothing** – The first thing to always make sure that you have in your car is a seasonally appropriate set of rugged clothing, including jeans, boots, hat, gloves, and coat.
- **Maps** – You should have both road and topographical maps of the entire area around where you live and work. The way you're used to getting home may not be usable at the time. Bridges can go down from earthquakes, and fires can cause other roads to be blocked by emergency equipment.
- **Roadside emergency kit** – Put together a kit of necessary tools to take care of your car should you break down along the way. This needs to include things like jumper cables, tire inflator, reflectors, jack, and lug wrench.

- **Tool kit** – You never know when you're going to need tools to fix your car in a breakdown or bust open a gate if you're locked in. Your basic tool kit doesn't have to be the best quality; they just need to be serviceable. Include pliers, wire cutters, combination wrenches, socket set (with ratchet), screwdrivers, electrical tape, duct tape, and a box cutter.
- **Safety absorbent** – If you're stuck in the ice and snow or your vehicle starts leaking gasoline, you're going to need something that can work either to give you traction or to soak up the spill before it catches fire. Sand and sawdust are commonly used for this, but one of the best materials available is kitty litter.

Statistics show that disasters will most likely happen during the daytime hours, so it makes sense to be prepared with items in your vehicle. This way, if you're away from home (and your loved ones) while the sun is up, you will have the support items in place to increase your odds of sleeping in your own bed that evening.

Chapter 5
WHY Be Prepared?

We've all grown up under a system which tells us that the government will take care of us if anything goes wrong. There's just one problem - the government has a very poor track record of doing that. FEMA, the government's principal agency for disaster relief, hasn't really learned from previous mistakes. It took *days* for them to get a team into New Orleans after Hurricane Katrina. When Hurricane Sandy hit New Jersey a few years later, FEMA didn't do much better. They didn't even purchase something as basic as water until the day after the hurricane hit!

Currently, FEMA, like many government organizations, spends more money than they bring in, having spent their entire budget on disasters that have already happened. When Hurricane Irma and Hurricane Maria hit Puerto Rico and

Florida in 2017, FEMA's budget was completely depleted for the next several years. More and more, people are coming to the realization that the government can't take care of their needs. Part of that is a general distrust of the federal government, but another part is that the social safety net has been stretched to the breaking point, and people are finally seeing it.

We've also seen a lot of social and political unrest during the same years as the pandemic, with a large number of protests turning into riots. While that may very well be because what was intended to be a peaceful protest was derailed by other groups who hijacked the protest to turn it into a riot, it still happened. There's always a chance of that happening again.

The high inflation that has followed the pandemic is threatening to turn into another recession. The gains that families made from receiving government stimulus checks have already turned into losses as inflation has eaten that money up. With continued financial pressure, we can expect to see continued unrest. Prepping can help you weather both the high prices and the high risk of living in a society that is on the edge of the breaking point.

We are living in a world where our national debt has topped 30 trillion dollars, yet Congress is spending money like there is no tomorrow. As long as that spending continues, we can't expect our economy to get back in order, let alone anything else.

Whether you believe in global warming or not, it's clear from looking at our history that the world has gone through both ice ages and warm spells. There have been times of flooding and of drought. If there's one thing we can be sure of, it's that weather is unpredictable.

At the time of this writing, both Lake Powell and Lake Mead, the nation's two largest reservoirs, are at their lowest historic levels. Scientists tell us that those lakes will never recover. At the same time, they are telling us that our aquifers are drying up. If we can't come up with enough water, not only will we face severe drought, but we'll have to deal with food shortages as well. Those shortages will hit the poor the hardest, as the wealthy can always spend whatever they need to get whatever they want.

At the same time that we're facing extreme drought and a risk to our food supplies, the population of the United States is growing by roughly 200,000 people per day. That's a lot of extra mouths to feed. How will we feed them with dwindling resources?

Why, then, do we prep? We prep because the best protection that any of us have is that which we can provide for ourselves. When we're prepared, we greatly increase the odds that our family will survive a catastrophic event, which is something that nobody else can do for us. Learning survival skills and building the necessary stockpile to survive is a clearer path to making sure our children grow up to have children of their own, even if the world changes considerably before they reach that age.

Community

One of the general philosophies that exist in the prepping community is the military concept of OPSEC (operational security). The basic idea is to not let people know what you're doing. This is important if you want to avoid having people show up at your doorstep looking for food and other necessities when the next disaster happens.

But there's a practical limit to that. Friends and family members who come into your home are likely to see your equipment and supplies. Neighbors will see things like gardens, water tanks, and solar panels. Most people won't make much of these things, but when a disaster happens and they're desperate, they'll remember that you are more prepared than they are. What are you going to do when they come knocking on your door?

Of course, just how quiet can you keep with those you love? If you truly love them and you're preparing for the inevitable disaster, wouldn't you want them to be prepared too? It's hard to turn away a family member when their kids are starving. So, unless you want to feed their kids, you'd better get them on board too.

In 2010, my wife and I built our first home and had our first babies. Responsibility for those young lives changed our perspective, giving us a new outlook on life. Shortly after moving into that home, there was a neighborhood barbecue, which gave us a great opportunity to meet our new neighbors.

Sometime during the evening, the conversation turned to what we would do in the event of a zombie apocalypse. It was kind of a fun conversation, feeding from the popularity of zombie movies and TV shows. It turned out that a lot of people in our neighborhood had useful skills which we would need should such a thing happen. I'm talking about people who could make bullets, a professional chef, a home-school mom, a home brewer, a nurse, a guy who was in the police academy, and a very handy DIYer who could do anything with his impressive collection of tools.

This became a common theme for those of us in the neighborhood, as we refined our plans through our gatherings. It went so far as to decide who to exclude from our "survival team" - people who had nothing to contribute or didn't want to contribute, but instead wanted the rest of us to take care of them.

Maybe this was all in fun, but I learned a valuable lesson from it. It's better to earn the neighbors' trust knowing they've got your back, rather than trying to stab you in it if things get bad. Maybe we weren't perfectly prepared for a disaster, but we at least had a plan to work together. I no longer live in that home and have lost contact with some of those people, but if I had to go through a disaster, that's the crew I'd want to have by my side.

Conclusion

Preppers are more than just people who are trying to escape from the system. They are people who have taken on the responsibility for their own lives. As such, they are some of the most important people a community can have. When things get bad, not only will they be taking care of themselves, but their communities will be able to depend on their knowledge and skills.

- **Preppers are part of the solution** – When a disaster strikes, not only will preppers be able to take care of themselves, they'll be looking out for others. The people rescuing those trapped by flood waters or giving food to the needy will most likely be preppers.
- **Preppers are ready for life's challenges** – We all face problems in our lives, whether it is a kid that

breaks his arm falling off the jungle gym or the loss of a job. These personal disasters are much easier for preppers to face because they are already prepared for much larger problems. Self-confidence comes from knowledge and preppers are constantly seeking more knowledge that can be applied in situations when others are at a loss.

- **Prepping brings peace, not turmoil** – People who don't know what to do tend to worry and panic. But just like in the military, those who have taken the time to learn what to do have no need to panic - they just fall back on their training.

- **Prepping builds up the community** – Preppers may not be the center of a community, but they strengthen any community. Prepping reaches across all ages, ethnicities, religions, and social divides. You can often find preppers in civic groups that help their community. That's just the kind of people they are: master gardeners, amateur radio operators, volunteer firemen, and others who help their neighbors.

- **Prepping promotes a good work ethic** – People who prep are less likely to be couch potatoes or to expect something to be handed to them for free. They work for what they have and expect life to be that way. Many go above and beyond what their employers expect of them, earning promotions.

- **Preppers are not dependent on the government –** One of the biggest identifying traits of the prepper is that they aren't expecting the government to bail them out when things go bad. Rather, they depend on their ability to deal with the situation and take care of themselves.
- **Preppers are resourceful –** Prepping teaches people a wide variety of skills, all of which are useful. When problems arise, even small ones, they know how to handle them, using their skills and tools to solve problems.
- **Prepping is cost-effective –** It's a whole lot cheaper to prepare for a disaster than it is to try and recover from one.

System #2 - PMA: Positive, Mental, Attitude

The Crucial Tactics You Must Learn for a Healthy Survival Mindset

"Everything can be taken away from a man but one thing: the last of human freedoms - to choose one's attitude in any given set of circumstances, to choose one's own way."

— Victor E. Frankl

A grandfather is speaking with his grandson and he tells him that, in life, there are two wolves inside all of us that are constantly at battle.

There's a good wolf, which represents traits like kindness, bravery, and love.

There's a bad wolf, which represents traits like greed, hatred, and fear.

The grandson processes this information for a minute, looks up at his grandfather, and asks "Well, Grandfather, which wolf wins?"

And the grandfather replies, "The one you feed!"

This parable of the two wolves relates to the human condition across the spectrum no matter who you are or where you are in your life. Which wolf are you feeding? In a survival situation, it's easy to drift toward negativity and let it weigh you down. However, the greatest impact you can make in your life and the lives of the people around you will come when your mind is in the right place.

Feed the good wolf so that kindness, bravery, and love win the day.

Maintaining a positive mental attitude (PMA) is important in ensuring even tiny victories. The U.S. military is a massive organization filled with some of the smartest tacticians and competent thinkers in the entire world. No matter which branch of the military, there are enormous amounts of money and energy poured into making sure that they have the best information possible, carefully researched and cross-checked to give our troops the optimal chances of winning and surviving.

With that in mind, it's interesting that every military manual that deals with survival starts out talking about having a positive mental attitude. The greatest experts the Department of Defense can find all agree that one's mental attitude has more to do with whether troops will survive than anything else.

Medical science is even recognizing this, as cancer patients with a positive mental attitude are more likely to survive their ordeal with cancer than those who are convinced that they're going to die.

Chapter 6
POSITIVE Mental Attitude

The idea of having a positive attitude has probably existed all through history, but it was Napoleon Hill, author of the book *Think and Grow Rich*, who recognized that how we think can affect our ability to succeed in life. While his understanding of this basic concept was focused on making money, the same principle applies to anything from sports, to getting a date, and on to survival.

For the purpose of survival, there are a few key things that a positive mental attitude does for us:

- **Focus** – Negativity saps your strength and resolve. A negative mind is a distracted mind. People who remain positive tend to stay focused on the task at hand, without jumping from problem to problem at any one point in time. This often generates higher quality outputs that are completed faster and where creative ideas flow easier. If you can keep yourself focused on the positive, it will motivate you to keep doing what's necessary, one step at a time, toward a successful finish. This applies both in a post-apocalyptic world as well as in your daily walk, so focus first!

- **Flexibility** – The quality to bend easily without breaking is crucial in how you choose to respond to most disaster situations. Your ability to change plans on the fly or modify your to-do tasks in emergency preparations will greatly increase your path to success. Bundle that with a willingness to compromise, and that could be the difference between life and death in a worst-case scenario event. Although failure is part of life, as well as part of survival prepping, if you remain flexible and keep your wits about you, your family will have a greater chance of pivoting away from that bad wolf, back toward that good wolf!

- **Connections** – Being positive about survival will attract others to you who are also positive about survival, helping you to build a team that will optimally work together to ensure common survival. Surround yourself with supportive people.

- **Self-confidence** – Perhaps the most important part of a positive mental attitude in the case of survival is confidence in yourself, which starts with being kind to yourself. The world is tough enough as it is; you don't need to constantly beat yourself up with negative self-talk. What soundtracks are running through your head? These are very powerful, especially in times of trauma or in an emergency. Keep your limiting beliefs at bay, change what you can, and stop comparing yourself to others. Positive self-talk will cause you to attempt things that you didn't know you could do and push through to succeed in doing them.

Emergency Conditioning

You can do a lot to help your mental attitude by playing scenarios through in your mind, deciding what you would do, and then imagining yourself doing them. This may seem hokey, but it is excellent training for your brain. Other than the muscle memory and conditioning that is needed to complete tasks, this mental exercise is some of the best training you can get without leaving the comfort of your own home.

This process is called "emergency conditioning" and is a process used by Navy SEALs. Before accomplishing a mission, SEALs go through the mission in their mind step-by-step and imagine everything that is likely to happen, as well as what can potentially go wrong. They find the solutions to those things that can go wrong in advance and record them in their memory. That way, when they encounter those problems, they aren't caught by surprise; rather, they already know how to respond to them. These warriors have rehearsed their tasks before battle and have such high confidence in the outcome, their mental state is nothing but positive. Their minds are clear, and their thinking is crisp, so their actions are swift and confident.

Your attitude literally determines your ability to survive. American POWs during the Korean War came up with the term "give-up-itis" (GUI) to refer to the destructive power of losing hope. Few who developed GUI actually survived their time in the POW camp and if they did, they were forever mentally scarred by it.

The biggest difference between an elite soldier and an average soldier is mindset. You truly can do whatever you put your mind to.

Chapter 7
Positive MENTAL Attitude

There are a lot of people out there who think that preppers are paranoid conspiracy theorists who wear tinfoil hats and are convinced that 5G is what caused COVID-19. Yes, there are preppers who are fearful and there are other preppers who are conspiracy theorists, but that doesn't account for the average prepper. The average prepper isn't anxious about something going wrong because they have a plan to deal with it when it does.

It is the people who don't know what they're going to do who panic. When the great toilet paper shortage of 2020 came, it wasn't preppers who were buying out the stores. They already had enough toilet paper.

One of the greatest survival instructors of our day, Cody Lundin, has been quoted as saying, "Survival is 90% psychology. When the chips are down, it doesn't matter what you have buried in the backyard or how many books on survival you've read. If you're a mental and emotional basket case during your survival episode, you're toast."[1]

Cody is right. You have to survive in your mind before you can survive in your body. That means having a plan and knowing that you can execute that plan. So, how do you do that?

Here are 6 important ideas to help improve PMA:

- **Gratitude** - Practicing gratitude will keep you grounded in the moment. It's important to focus on and appreciate the things that we often take for granted. Reflect on how fortunate you are when something good happens - and even when it feels like *nothing* good is happening. Counting your blessings as they come is infectious - it will help the people around you remain positive.
- **Self-Compassion** - The next time you're having a pity party, criticizing your decision-making or your ability to complete a tough task, ask yourself: "Would I talk this way to my best friend?" There will be setbacks, failures, and mistakes in prepping. Don't beat yourself up. Learn from your mistakes as quickly as possible and move on.
- **Faith** - Belief in a higher power will be a massive aid in a survival situation. In both positive and difficult

times, your faith is your rock to lean on. It's as simple as that.

- **Willpower** - A large part of willpower involves increasing your ability to deal with pressure by planning and learning to manage stress. You can do this by challenging yourself, controlling your impulses, and delaying gratification - and good habits are sure to follow.

- **Visualization** - Imagine that you have the skills and materials necessary to fulfill your basic needs. Visualize the accomplishment of the productive tasks that need to be handled each day. Think of your goals and dreams for your family. Keep in mind that visualization can also work against you if you're filling your head with doubt, fear, and things you cannot control. Over time, mental imagery will form muscle memory, which will strengthen your emotional IQ.

- **Just Start** - Sometimes, simply starting a task can feel overwhelming. There will be numerous challenges and obstacles facing you in an emergency crisis, so get rid of the all-or-nothing mentality. Engage in a task, even if you have to force yourself to begin. Once you get the ball rolling, you might not want to stop. You just have to take that first step.

Another important part of mental preparation is developing your mental toughness, which gives you the grit, character, and perseverance to perform under pressure in any conditions you may find yourself in.

This is different from physical toughness, which comes from exercise and exposing your body to hardship. Of the two, mental toughness is more important. Lack of physical toughness may cause your body to fail at a critical moment, but lack of mental toughness will cause you to quit long before your body does.

So, just how do you improve your mental toughness? By challenging yourself. It doesn't matter what you challenge yourself to do, just as long as it is something that you don't normally do. Make yourself do it beyond the point that you think you can. When you feel like quitting, make yourself do it a little bit more. If that's lifting weights with your non-dominant hand, then do three or four more repetitions than you thought you could. If that's standing on one leg, stand there a couple more minutes than you thought was possible. If it's conditioning yourself to withstand the cold, then go out without a jacket, keeping yourself warm from activity.

In 1971, Juliane Koepcke, a 17-year-old girl, was flying out from her parents' research station over the Peruvian rainforest. Their plane was struck by lightning and literally came apart. After somehow miraculously surviving a two-mile fall, Juliane found herself alone in the jungle and had to walk out alone. Although unprepared, improperly dressed, and injured, she started walking, mostly staying in the creek, which she knew would be safer. Finally, ten days later and nearly delirious, she found a boat and then a cabin, where she spent the night. The next morning, she heard voices outside and knew she was rescued.

It was Juliane's mental toughness that allowed her to survive, not her preparedness. The only item she took from that plane crash was a bag of candy, which didn't last her long. She didn't even have a pair of shoes, as she lost one while falling through the air. Yet she took the other one and used it to probe ahead of her, looking for snakes hiding in the leaves. Had it not been for her resourcefulness and mental toughness, she would have perished.

Chapter 8
Positive Mental ATTITUDE

Not all preppers are created alike. Some do the minimum they feel they need to do in order to gain a sense of security; however, most decide to go much further than that, continuing to improve their family's security. As we can see from the story of Juliane Koepcke in the last chapter, it's not all about what survival gear you have and how big a stockpile of supplies you have, it's about having the knowledge and attitude to survive.

Motivational speakers love to say, "Your attitude determines your altitude." There's probably nowhere that phrase applies more than in survival. Another way of looking at that is that your attitude is going to affect what you do, and that's going to affect your chances at survival.

If you're going to have a positive mental attitude during a time of crisis, you're going to have to work on your attitude in general. You can't be negative all the time and then expect to be positive when you're caught in a survival situation. Rather, you're going to have to train yourself to have a positive attitude all the time, so that it is in your very nature to be positive, even when everyone else is screaming, "We're going to die!"

So the question is: How do you change your attitude from negative to positive?

This answer is going to seem simplistic, but it works. The starting point is to fill your mind with positive things. The saying "garbage in, garbage out" definitely applies to attitude. An upward spiral of positive emotion occurs when your head is full of positive thoughts. When you smile, neuropeptides that work toward fighting off stress flood your brain and, in turn, increase your happiness. Keep your attitude out of the trash and clean results are likely to follow.

Have you ever noticed how really active people tend to be positive, while people who spend their lives as couch potatoes tend toward negativity? On the other hand, people who are learning or doing are generally positive. They see the results of their actions and they see their life improving. This has a positive effect on their attitude, which helps those people to be more prepared to survive.

Exercise is great for building a positive attitude. That doesn't mean that you have to get a gym membership, join a golf league, or start running. There are a lot of simple exercises that you can do right at home, which will build up your body, helping you feel better. For that matter, you can get a lot of exercise just working around your home and yard. Landscaping can be pretty physical, just as remodeling can. Both benefit your family and add value to your home.

Keep your mind active too. If you aren't an avid reader, become one. Reading is the basis of all education. Just about everything mankind has learned in the last 100 years is written down somewhere, whether in a book or on the internet. Find a comfy chair and read. Build your library of books, making sure that you have plenty of books that will help you when it comes time to survive.

None of us can learn everything and become an expert about it, but with books, you can have an expert on tap whenever you need one. Having a robust reference section of physical books in your own home library will come in handy. Real paper books won't be lost, like the internet could be, in the event of losing electrical power.

Your library can be an important part of your family's survival, especially if you fill it with books that tell you how to do things that you don't already know how to do. There are a lot of military and home repair manuals, as well as cookbooks and food preservation books, that are available for free online. Just print them out and put them in binders to increase your library on the cheap.

It isn't so much what you do as it is that you do *something* to make your life better, whether it's cognitive, physical, or creative. The idea is that taking up a new activity will improve your quality life, thus generating a more positive attitude.

Here are some possible activities:

- Learn to dance
- Go fishing
- Build a piece of survival gear
- Learn a foreign language
- Read a personal growth book
- Remodel part of your home
- Learn a new survival skill
- Go hiking
- Learn how to do something you always wanted to, but never did
- Play a sport
- Learn how to cook
- Write a story
- Go to the mountains
- Make up a joke and share it
- Start a new hobby
- Learn a lost skill that might be useful in a post-disaster world, like blacksmithing

Conclusion

What good is preparing for disasters by stockpiling food, equipment, and other supplies without preparing yourself mentally? No matter how big your stockpile and how much survival gear you have, it will eventually run out. Whether or not you survive at that point will depend more on having the right mental attitude than anything else.

Having a positive mental attitude can make up for a lot of shortcomings in other areas of preparedness. That's not to say we shouldn't prepare beyond developing that attitude; rather, that attitude should end up being what motivates the rest of it. As we work on our attitude, everything else that we do will seem easier and make more sense. We will do our prepping tasks with joy, learning new skills and securing our family's future.

System #3 - IDEA: Identify, Develop, Execute, Analyze

The Life-saving Acronym for Long-term Survival

"It might be dusty and hidden away, but it is there some-where inside you: the heart of a survivor. Courage. Tenacity. Strength. So don't shy away from the hard times; they are your chance to shine. Struggle develops strength and storms make you stronger."

— Bear Grylls

There's an old saying that failing to plan is planning to fail. The big thing that separates preppers from everyone else is that we have a plan to deal with the disasters that life tends to bring. Everything else we do, like stockpiling food, is based upon that plan.

But there's no one-size-fits-all plan for prepping. Every individual and every family has a unique situation. While we all have some things in common, we live in different parts of the country that are prone to different natural disasters, our children are of different ages, we have different health and diet needs, we have different levels of training and understanding, and our budgets are different. If I were to hand you my survival plan and expect you to use it, the first thing you'd have to do is change it to fit your needs.

The training contained in this book will give you the ability to develop your own plan and execute that plan to perfection. Your family will become more secure because you will be one of the few families in your neighborhood, if not the only one, who is ready for whatever life brings your way. That's a gift you can give your family that nobody else can.

Chapter 9
IDENTIFY Prepping Needs

Before you do anything to prepare, it's a good idea to know just what it is that you're preparing for. You could just say, "I'm preparing for a disaster," but just what sort of disaster? It isn't going to do you any good to prepare for a hurricane if you live in the middle of Kansas, nor is it going to do much good to prepare for a winter blizzard if you live in Hawaii. Each region of the country is prone to its own types of disasters, even though we all share some of the same risks.

Then there are the disasters that can hit us all, like the COVID-19 pandemic. Who would have guessed that we would all be living under lockdown conditions due to a virus? While pandemics are real, we simply don't expect them.

Back in 2014, there was a major outbreak of Ebola, one of the scariest viral diseases on the face of the Earth, with a much higher mortality rate than COVID. Not only did thousands of people die from the disease, but the disease managed to make it all the way to the U.S. thanks to air travel. Fortunately, not many people were infected here in the U.S., but the risk was present. Even scarier was the risk that some terrorist organization would get their hands on the virus and use it for bioterrorism.

The risk was bad enough to motivate me to prepare for a serious epidemic reaching my community. While I didn't end up needing masks, gloves, hand sanitizer, and even hazardous material suits back in 2014, it put me way ahead of everyone else when COVID came along. I had no need to hunt for all of the necessary personal protection equipment at that time because I already had it. If you recall, many of these items were nearly impossible to find on the store shelves, or online, so being prepared with owning this gear was helpful.

So just what sort of risks face us today? These fall into a few basic categories:

- Family emergencies - financial, health, death, etc.
- Natural disasters
- Financial disasters - inflation, recession, financial collapse, etc.
- War-related disasters

- Man-made disasters - chemical spills and leaks, fire, etc.
- Loss of infrastructure
- Another pandemic
- Zombie apocalypse or alien invasion (well… maybe not)

In your own mind, you should be able to come up with a guess as to just how likely each of these is to happen and just how serious it would be to deal with. Grade them from 1 to 5 in each of these areas. For example, people living in Florida might put hurricanes high on their list of probable disasters, so that would be a 5 for likelihood. On the other hand, they may be so used to dealing with hurricanes, having built their homes to withstand them, that they feel that the potential damage from a hurricane is slight, rating it as a 2 for seriousness.

Once we do that for all of the potential disasters we can think of, we can add up the scores for each of them. Going back to our Florida example, the two scores for hurricanes add up to 7. Compared to that, they might feel that the risk of war affecting their state is a 1, with a potential seriousness of 3. That adds up to 4. So, of the two scenarios, preparing for a hurricane is much more important than preparing for a war.

We can do this with all potential disasters, giving ourselves a realistic idea of what we should be preparing for.

There's another part of this that will affect your personal survival plan - where you live. People who live in the city have a different survival situation than those living in the country. Those who rent apartments have different things to contend with than those who own their homes. Nearby geographical features, like rivers and forests, can be valuable sources of necessary supplies, such as water and firewood. On the other hand, these same features can be a detriment - rivers can flood and forests can burn.

Make sure you understand how the basic systems of your home function. Can you shut off the water or gas if there's a leak? Do you have a generator for backup power should the lights go out? If your water comes from a well, do you have a manual way of pumping water in the case of a well pump failure or blackout, which would kill the power you need for that pump?

Any survival necessity needs to have a backup. As it's said in the prepping community, "Two is one and one is none." Having a backup, even if it isn't as good as the original, ensures that your family has essential resources to survive.

What about your home itself - how sturdy is it? What condition is your roof in? Are there decorative items on the outside of the home, such as shutters, which could blow off during high winds? When disaster strikes, it's easy to forget that your home itself may get damaged, so you'll want to be prepared to make some emergency repairs.

Chapter 10
Chapter 10 - DEVELOP Your Plan

Now that you understand the risks that you're facing and what you have to work with, it's time to start developing a survival plan for your family. It's easy to be flippant at this point and say, "My plan is to survive." But just what does that mean to you? In other words, what level of loss is acceptable to ensure that your family survives?

If you own a business, can you sacrifice that business to ensure your family's survival or is that business essential to your family to the point where you have to make sure that it survives as well? What about livestock - can you live without them if the disaster takes them? Can you survive if your home gets destroyed in a natural disaster? All of these, and much more, are important parts of creating a solid survival plan.

It's necessary to get your family involved in survival planning as well. They may not be interested or see the need for it, or they may be too nervous to consider that a disaster could happen, but you need their buy-in. Tornadoes, EMPs, earthquakes - any disaster that strikes will affect them too.

Many people make the mistake of starting their plan under the assumption that everyone is at home. There's one huge problem with this - it's a fantasy. Rarely are all the members of a household at home unless the disaster strikes at 4:00 in the morning. Your starting point needs to assume that everyone is scattered out, doing the activities that keep us busy every day.

With that being the case, the first step in your survival plan is for someone to develop a blueprint that works best for your family and home. Who is going to do what? How will they communicate? What should everyone do when they get that message? This will likely be to head for home, but in that case, who will pick up those who don't drive but are too far to walk? How will you get the kids out of school? Can they start walking home and get picked up along the way? Are they of an age where they could slip out of class without a parent having to be there to pick them up?

As part of your communications plan, designate someone outside of the family (and preferably outside the area) as a point of contact for everyone to use. This person can be part of your extended family or a friend. The important thing is that this person needs to be someone that everyone can contact easily.

But what do you do if your cell phones are out? The cellular system is pretty reliable, but it can fail. In such a case, everyone in the family needs to have a laminated list of emergency numbers, including each other and your designated out-of-town point of contact. Nobody bothers to learn phone numbers anymore, so if your phone battery is dead, there is no way of communicating.

The Red Cross has developed a free emergency app that you and your family members can download from the app store. Among other features, it has an "I'm Safe" button, which family members can use to let the rest of the family know that they're safe in the event of a disaster. A more secure and private option is to use their safe and well website, which can be found at: www.redcross.org/safeandwell.[1]

Once you're all at home, what are you going to do? Depending on the severity of the disaster, you may have to do many things that are not part of your everyday life, like keeping a fire going and getting water from your rainwater capture system. Who is going to be the responsible person to do each of those tasks? How will you all work together to ensure your family's survival?

Keep in mind that you will probably need to put some sort of rationing scheme into place. If the only water you have available is from a rainwater capture system, you can't afford to have anyone taking 45-minute showers. Besides, the shower may not be working anyway. Food will likely need to be rationed as well, especially if it turns into a long-term survival situation.

While your main plan will probably be to stay at home, bugging in, you also want to be ready to bug out should that need arise. Should you need to bug out, it will probably need to happen quickly, requiring that you're ready to move in a moment's notice. This means having a complete plan for evacuation: Where are you going to go? How are you going to get there? What's the route? Do you have that route and alternates marked on a map? Do you have everything that you'll need packed into ready-to-grab bags? Do you have a checklist to make sure nothing gets left behind? We'll be discussing this in depth in System #9.

Chapter 11
EXECUTE with Confidence

Planning is critical to your family's survival, and the more detailed your plans are and the more things you've thought about ahead of time, the better. Will everything go according to your plan? Absolutely not. But believe it or not, the human mind tends to shut down in emergency situations, right when you need it working at its peak. By having a written plan to reference, you've got a starting point. Yes, you'll likely have to modify it at some point, but at least you have something to work with.

Ezra Taft Benson, former president of The Church of Jesus Christ of Latter-day Saints, said this: "It is easier to prepare and prevent, than to repair and repent." He practices what he preaches, not only by being prepared himself, but by teaching the 16 million people in his church to do so as well.

The Latter-day Saints are the biggest community of preppers there is.

You're going to need to be able to execute that written plan as well. This means developing the skills necessary to do the things you say you're going to do. If you are planning on heating your home with wood when the power goes out, but you don't know how to start a fire or split a log, you're going to be in trouble. There are a lot of skills associated with survival, and you need to spend some time learning as many as you can. Not only that, but you need to teach them to your family as well.

We'll be talking about a lot of these necessary skills throughout the rest of this book, but a few things that aren't going to be discussed that should still be considered are as follows:

- Beekeeping - if you live in an area where you can keep bees
- Baking and breadmaking
- Cooking from scratch
- Construction, including plumbing, electrical work, and even masonry
- Hunting and fishing
- Knitting
- Sewing, including repurposing clothing
- Welding and possibly even blacksmithing
- Saving seeds from your garden

- Rope skills
- Sharpening a knife and other tools by hand

It's a good idea to run disaster drills with your family, setting aside a time when you'll be doing things as you would if a real disaster were to strike. These drills should include various different types of disasters, as well as different parts of the infrastructure failing. Some might start with everyone at home, while others have everyone at school and work. It's also a good idea to run a bug-out drill as well.

Disaster drills perform two main functions for you. First, they give your family a chance to practice doing the things you're planning on doing so that they're not being done for the first time in the midst of a disaster. This will build their confidence, as well as provide necessary training. The second thing they will do is highlight weaknesses in your plans so that you can make necessary changes and adjustments to improve your plans.

Remember, survival situations can happen anytime, anywhere. In 1971, the Robertson family set out on a wooden schooner and headed to parts unknown in what the father of the family called part of the "university of life." For 17 months, the family sailed from port to port, seeing the world. But in 1972, the family encountered a pod of killer whales off the coast of the Galapagos Islands. The whales attacked their boat, severely damaging it. The family escaped in a lifeboat with only a 6-day supply of food. Over a month later, the family was finally rescued by Japanese fishermen. They had survived on rainwater and sea turtles that they'd captured. Even though everything had been going fine up to that point and they weren't expecting that attack, they were well enough prepared and trained that they were able to survive not only the attack, but living in the lifeboat for all that time with limited resources.

Making a Prepping Budget

It may already be sounding to you like prepping can get expensive, and we're just getting started. Yes, prepping can be costly, but nobody is suggesting that you buy everything now. Those of us who have been preppers for years have spread the cost of prepping out over that time; you can and should do the same.

Start by looking at the budget you already have. There are 3 possible budget levels that you have to work with: totally broke, small budget, or large budget. Then figure out which one of them you are currently living under. If you're living under anything but the "totally broke" level, you can probably afford to set aside a little bit of money each month in order to prepare.

For most of us, it's easier to build a stockpile by increasing what we're already buying by a small amount every month. In other words, don't just have a jar of spaghetti sauce or a box of cereal in the pantry; buy two or three. Add additional items you currently use (and would still use in an emergency) each time you go to the grocery store. You'll be surprised at how quickly your pantry will fill up with real food (not junk food) that you enjoy eating, but that you'll also be able to eat during a time of emergency.

Take advantage of sales when you're buying your food and other supplies. I ran into a sale on boxed macaroni and cheese a year ago, so I bought a whole case. That may sound excessive, but it only cost me $2.40, since it was a throwback sale at $0.10 a box!

A good rule of thumb is to use the same rule that the grocery store uses. It's called "first in, first out," meaning that, when you buy a new box of cereal or jar of spaghetti sauce, you don't put it in front of the one that's already there; you put the new behind the old so that the oldest one is always in front and will get used first. This system will help ensure that you don't have any food that you have to throw away because it has gotten too old.

You can save a lot of money by making your own food rather than buying it. It's hard to beat the supermarket price for canned fruits and vegetables, but you can make your own granola, hot chocolate, candles, and firestarters for a fraction of the cost you'd pay for commercial ones. There are many more things, from pre-packaged foods to survival gear, that preppers have figured out how to make for themselves.

Here's a good example: Firewood is a supply you should never have to pay for. There are always dead trees in peoples' yards that need to come down, or tree limbs that have been blown down by a storm. Be a community-minded citizen and offer to cut those trees up and haul them off. They don't need to know that you're doing it so that you can get free firewood. For that matter, many people will even pay you for gathering *your* firewood from *their* yards.

Don't forget gifts. Everyone, in every family, struggles to come up with gift ideas for family members. You can solve that problem for your entire family by giving them a list of survival gear that you'd love to receive. Just make sure that it has items that fit every budget so that they won't be tempted to buy you another bottle of cologne instead.

Chapter 12
ANALYZE the Results

Now that you have a plan put together, you can sit back and revel in a job well done, right? Wrong. The thing about plans is that they need constant updating. Your situation is going to change, as is your knowledge and the resources you have to work with. As you grow in your knowledge, you'll discover things in your survival plan that just aren't going to work the way you thought. Children are going to grow and gain the ability to take on more complex tasks in a survival situation.

When Hurricane Harvey struck, flooding southeast Houston, a friend of mine was living in an area that could be considered a hurricane zone. Even so, he was far enough from the coast and high enough in elevation that they thought they didn't have to worry about flooding. However, the area his family lived in was extremely flat, so water wouldn't run off any better than it did in Houston. He quickly realized that since he didn't have a boat, he would have been just like one of those families in Louisiana, waiting for the Cajun Navy[1] to rescue him, if that hurricane had stalled over the area he lived in.

My friend's solution was not to go out and buy a new fishing boat, although that would have been nice. Rather, he bought an inflatable rubber boat so that his family could self-evacuate if the need arose. While it wouldn't have been the most comfortable evacuation, it would have given them the ability to get to higher ground if the water got too high to drive through. There are always lessons that we can learn, even if the situation seems totally different than anything we might encounter.

Prepping is a process rather than an event. You'll need to be checking how you're doing on a regular basis. This means checking your stockpile of food, water, and other supplies; checking the survival gear that you have; and checking how well your home is prepared to weather a crisis. Gear and supplies can go bad, so don't just check inventory - make sure that it's still in usable condition.

There's another part of analysis as well - self-analysis. We need to be checking on ourselves, looking to see how ready we are to survive. This means analyzing our mental state, the skills we've learned, our physical condition, and our health. There are a lot of people in the prepping community who honestly aren't prepared to survive. They're overweight, have high blood pressure, are on medications for chronic conditions, and are out of shape. If they had to bug out on foot, they might be able to make it only 3 or 4 miles per day.

If you have any chronic health conditions, take care of them now, before a crisis comes. For that matter, there are several medical check-ups that you should be getting regularly, if you aren't already. If you consider good health as part of being prepared, then chronic conditions aren't just health issues, they're survival issues for you and your family. Possible medical check-ups include:

- **Annual health check-up** – This gives your doctor a chance to see if anything is going wrong, which is especially important as you age.
- **Chronic disease follow-up** – If you have diabetes, high blood pressure, or any of the other chronic conditions that plague modern society, you need to follow up regularly with your doctor to see how your treatment regimen is working. Your doctor may be satisfied with simple maintenance, but you should be seeking a solution so that you don't need to be on medications for the rest of your life.
- **Cancer screening** – Both men and women need to be screened regularly for cancer, making sure that this killer hasn't entered their body. It's much easier and cheaper to deal with cancer early on than to wait until it takes over.

- **Mental health** – We can all use an occasional mental health check, especially if we've been through any stressful, life-changing events. Life can hit us with some heavy blows, and we need to know that we've recovered from them; otherwise, they might crop up to haunt us at inopportune times.

As you age, these check-ups are more important than ever. Our bodies tend to deteriorate over time, especially if we don't take care of them. Things that we could shake off when younger can have a major impact once we top half a century. Regardless, the sooner we know about any problems, the sooner we can get a handle on making them go away.

Common Mistakes to Avoid

In prepping, there are some very common mistakes that people make. While these are not all the mistakes that are made, they are the most common:

- **Not stockpiling equipment as well as food** – It's easy to become so focused on building a good stockpile that we overlook having the survival gear necessary to go with that food. How are you going to cook that food with the electricity out? Do you have an alternate method? How are you going to purify water? Can you start a fire without using a torch or gasoline to get it going?

- **Going "gear crazy"** – As the prepping community has grown, so has the commercial opportunity of selling to the prepping niche. This has led to a multitude of new products made just for preppers. Unfortunately, it has also led to a lot of gimmick products, which are there more to take your money than to help you survive. While you do need gear, make sure you truly need something before buying it. Then, when you do buy, buy the best quality you can afford. It will last longer, which could save your life.

- **Overlooking family medical conditions** – We live in a society where most of us have sedentary lifestyles, sitting in front of a computer during the day and in front of a television at night. This has led to a nationwide obesity epidemic, along with weight-related diseases like hypertension and diabetes. People with these conditions can survive, but you've got to prepare for them. If any family member has special medical needs, such as prescription drugs, those have to be part of your prep too.

- **Forgetting their four-legged friends** – If you have pets or livestock, you've got to prep for them as well. What's your pup going to eat? If you don't have a stockpile of dog food, then he'll either starve or end up eating the meat your family needs. If you're raising any sort of livestock, from chickens to goats, make sure you have the medications they might need, or you'll lose that source of food.

- **Improper storage** – Most of the food we purchase in the supermarket is not packaged for long-term storage. Other than canned goods, just about everything is packaged with the idea that it will be consumed within a couple of months. If it's kept longer, it will get stale. Worse than that, bugs can get into most of it, rendering it unusable. There are safe ways of repackaging food, but it is essential that everything used is properly cleaned to ensure that there are no bacteria inside to contaminate the food.

Conclusion

Every emergency organization and every country's military have people whose full-time job is to develop emergency plans. These organizations recognize the importance of those plans, knowing that when the time comes and a worst-case scenario event occurs, there isn't time to think - there's only time to react.

Taking the time to develop detailed plans and look at every possible contingency may seem like a waste of time, especially since things never work out as we expect, but history shows us that it's not a waste of time. Those who *have* a plan are better able to reach their goals even if they have to deviate from that plan. It is said that no plan ever survives the first encounter with the enemy, but the truth is that much more of that plan survives than most people realize.

The same will happen for you as you develop your own plan. When disaster strikes, it may seem that all plans go out the window, but even just parts of your plan will work as an outline for what you need to do, and that makes the work worth the effort.

System #4 - KISS: Keep It Simple, Stupid

Building Your Prepper's Pantry

"Fortune favors the prepared mind."

— Louis Pasteur

Most preppers start their journey by beginning to stockpile food, which makes sense, especially in the light of the shortages that we all saw happen in 2020 during the COVID-19 pandemic. When we think about having to survive, it's natural for food to be one of the first things we think about. We've all just had a great lesson in how fragile our supply lines are.

I remember watching the supermarket shelves empty out in the early days of the pandemic. It was alarming seeing just how fast the stores emptied out from the mild panic people were feeling. Dealing with a more pressing panic would be even worse, looking more like Black Friday, with people fighting to get what they want.

If you're thinking of solely living off the land in the case of a disaster, think again. Any situation that would make you think you need to hunt for food will also put a lot of other people in the same situation. The game supply will quickly be overwhelmed by hunters, thinning out animal populations and making food scarce.

The solution is having a stockpile of food that you can use, which will both keep long-term and provide proper nourishment to your family should a disaster strike. You'll also need to consider how you're going to cook that food if your normal means of cooking is unavailable.

Chapter 13
KEEP: Stock Food You Like to Eat and Know How to Cook

Building a food stockpile is more than just buying a lot of food. You could do that, but you'll undoubtedly end up buying some of the wrong things. Worse, you will probably miss buying some of the things you need. Some of the most important food items are easily overlooked.

What do I mean by that? Most of us buy a lot of fresh, frozen, and junk foods as part of our normal grocery budget. Obviously fresh food isn't going to last long, and frozen food might not either if you lose power. However, that doesn't mean that you shouldn't buy any frozen food at all, since you'll need it for your day-to-day eating. For your stockpile, though, you're better off concentrating on shelf-stable foods.

You may need to come up with new recipes to cook those foods and learn some new cooking methods, especially if you're not used to making them part of your family's diet. If you've never baked bread, now is a good time to learn - it's not actually all that hard. Don't wait until a disaster happens to try it; you need to do your experimenting now, a little bit at a time, so that you don't overwhelm your family with food they don't like.

First, let's get your current food pantry organized so when you begin adding to the stockpile you know where to find things. Unless you're accustomed to having several months' worth of food in your home, you probably aren't ready to store it. That food will take up a lot of room and you're better off if it's well-organized. Otherwise, you won't know what you have on hand, so when you do need to use that food, you won't be able to find what you need.

Before rushing off to the store, take some time to think about just how much food you're going to be stockpiling. Most people start out with a small stockpile, enough to feed their families for 2 to 3 months. Over time, they add to that supply to build a larger stockpile, which can provide for their needs over a year or more. A good way to do this is to build a three-tier stockpile:

- **Tier 1 (1 to 3 months)** – This level of stockpiling will get you through pretty much all natural disasters and the time it takes for the supply chain to be reestablished. As long as you restock this pantry when you do your regular food shopping, every week or two, then it can remain as that first tier without being diminished. If your kitchen has a large enough pantry, this can be kept in your kitchen and can serve as the food that you use on a regular basis.

- **Tier 2 (3 to 6 months)** – This level of food stockpile is enough to provide for your family in the case of a larger disaster, where it may take longer for the supply chain to be reestablished. You're not going to be working out of this stockpile, so you'll want the food packaged for long-term storage. If you have a basement, that's the ideal storage environment.
- **Tier 3 (6 months to 2 years)** – The idea of having such a long-term supply of food is to provide your family with enough to eat in the case of a TEOTWAWKI event during the time that you are planting and getting your food production up and running. This should also be stored in the basement, preferably separate from Tier 2 and in a more hidden area. That way, if anyone breaks in, they might not see all that you have.

The amount of food that it takes to sustain a family for 12 months or more is surprisingly large. To figure out just how much, it's best to create a 2- or 3-week menu and build a shopping list from that. The next step is to multiply it by 26 in order to figure out how much of any given item you'll need to have to last a year. Keep in mind that you likely won't be able to buy things like bread, so you'll need to bake your own. Remember, detail is important; things like ketchup, salt, and spices are items easy to overlook, but are an essential part of your stockpile. Check out our handy family prepper pantry food calculator spreadsheet that comes free with the purchase of this book!

Building and Organizing Your Prepper Pantry

The layout of your stockpile pantry will be largely dictated by the space you have available. It's best to keep food and containers off the floor to protect them from water, although 5-gallon plastic buckets can sit on the floor since they are waterproof.

Buy or build sturdy shelves, keeping in mind that there will be a lot of weight stacked on them. Anchor those shelves to the floor and walls or to the floor joists overhead so that they won't move in an earthquake.

You'll see designs of item-specific storage racks online as DIY projects for preppers. These might be great for organization and especially for maintaining a FIFO (first in, first out) food supply. However, unless you have a lot of space to devote to your food supply, you'll find that those organizers take up too much space relative to the amount of food that they can hold. In most cases, you're better off building generic food storage shelves so that you can move things around as your stockpile grows.

Keeping your stockpile organized is important. Things that go together should be stored together as much as possible so that you can easily see how much of them are available. You may have a lot of empty space on your shelves at the beginning, as you should save that empty space to use when you buy more of those items.

5 Enemies of Food Shelf-Life

We aren't the only ones who want to eat the food in our pantries; there are plenty of other critters who think that any food is there for their enjoyment. They don't understand the concept of ownership and aren't going to be bothered by any sign you put up telling them to keep out.

But it's not only critters - the environment can be hard on our food supplies as well, causing nutrients to oxidize and eliminating their nutritional value. Here is a list of enemies to our food stockpile:

- Heat
- Light
- Moisture - attacks both the food and the packaging
- Pests - bacteria, insects, rodents, and more
- Oxygen

Because of these enemies, it's a good idea to avoid storing food in the garage or attic. Basements work well as long as they don't flood. They're cool, usually dark, and most people use them for storage anyway.

The food we buy and how it is packaged is also something to consider. Any food that we buy for long-term storage needs to be shelf-stable and not require refrigeration. Canned food will last for years, regardless of the best-by date stamped on the can, but most of the other food we buy, especially dry foods, are not usually packaged for long-term storage. Some foods go stale after a few months, and other foods can be invaded by insects and rodents. These foods need to be repackaged to maintain a long shelf life. In a later chapter, we'll dive into how to repackage that food to last for several years.

Chapter 14
IT: It's All About the Food on Hand

The only food that matters when a disaster strikes is the food you have on hand. As we all saw when people started to panic over the coronavirus, it doesn't take long for the grocery stores to empty out, and it can take a long time for them to get stocked back up again. Of course, in a TEOTWAWKI event, the stores may never be restocked. In either case, we've got to be able to feed our families.

Building a food stockpile means finding shelf-stable foods that will provide your family with adequate nutrition. Most people concentrate on a high-carbohydrate diet, which is fine, as we'll all be doing lots of physical work to burn those carbohydrates off. But be sure to include enough fats and proteins as well. Protein is especially important, as the body needs it for building new cells.

While different people put different things into their stock-piles, you're going to want to consider including:[1]

Grains and other carbohydrates:

- White rice
- Wheat flour and other flours for baking - whole grains store better for long-term use
- Baking supplies - baking powder, baking soda, vanilla extract, etc.
- Cornmeal
- Popcorn
- Pasta
- Quinoa
- Instant mashed potatoes
- Oatmeal, cream of wheat, and grits

Fats:

- Shortening
- Cooking oil - vegetable, olive, etc.
- Peanut butter - also a great source of protein

Proteins:

- Canned meats and fish of all kinds
- Textured vegetable protein (TVP)
- Dehydrated meats - can be rehydrated for use in soups

- Freeze-dried meats
- Shelf-stable dry-cured bacon
- Cured meats
- Nuts
- Dried beans of all kinds

Fruits and vegetables:

- Canned fruits
- Canned vegetables
- Dried fruits

Other food items:

- Salt - necessary both as a dietary supplement and to preserve food
- Spices - if you find yourself eating foods you're not accustomed to, at least you can flavor it like your favorite comfort food
- Spaghetti sauce - anything with spaghetti sauce on it tastes like spaghetti
- Powdered milk - for baking
- Powdered eggs - also for baking
- Cornstarch - for thickening things like gravy
- Sugar and/or honey - both keep indefinitely
- Flavoring extracts
- Stock or bouillon
- Coffee and/or tea

- Hard candies

Please note that, while this list is fairly extensive, you're going to want to add items that your family likes or that are ingredients for meals your family enjoys. It is not intended to be a complete list, just a starting point.

Long-Term Storage of Dried Foods

As I mentioned earlier, the dried foods that we buy in the grocery store aren't usually packaged for long-term storage. They are intended to be used within a few months. So, to make them part of our food stockpile, they need to be repackaged. A common method for doing this is to use 5-gallon plastic buckets lined with aluminized mylar bags. Adding oxygen absorbers inside the bags will greatly increase the shelf life of some of these foods.

Make sure you have a lot of food on hand when doing this. Most people fill an entire 5-gallon bucket with the same type of food, although it is possible to put multiple types if several mylar bags are used.

1. Open 6-gallon aluminized mylar bags and place them in the buckets.
2. Fill the bags with food to about 1 inch below the bucket's rim.
3. Label the buckets in several places.

4. Using a hair straightener or clothes iron, heat seal the bags, leaving about 2 inches open at one end.

5. Working quickly, place an oxygen absorber in the bag, then suck out as much air as possible with a vacuum cleaner hose, taking care to not suck out the food.

6. Seal the top of the bag the rest of the way.

7. Fold the bag flap over and close the bucket.

There are many sources for 5-gallon buckets, including your local home-improvement center. They may even have food-grade buckets, which are white for easy identification. The mylar bags and oxygen absorbers are available from a number of online suppliers.

Oxygen absorbers are very fast-acting, hence the need for working quickly when that point is reached in the process. It can be helpful to have an assistant who is responsible for dealing with the oxygen absorbers, allowing you to concentrate on sealing the bags.

Other Items to Consider Storing

You can create what feels like an endless list of items to add to your stockpile. The more you prepare, the more things you'll find that you want to add. There are a few things I'd like to point out that may otherwise be forgotten.

Seed Vault

Since you'll need to grow your own food in a long-term survival situation, you will want to buy or build a seed vault. This is a collection of seeds that you can use to grow fruits and vegetables. Ideally, they should be vacuum-packed and stored in the freezer to help keep them fresh.

The most important consideration for your seed vault is the type of seeds you are storing. The only type that's practical for survival is heirloom seeds. These are the original varieties of the various types of fruits and vegetables. There are literally thousands of varieties available, although you may need to buy them from an heirloom seed bank rather than from your local garden center.

The main reason you want heirloom seeds is that the seeds that grow on those plants can be harvested and saved for the next year, allowing you to keep your garden growing perpetually. Hybrid seeds won't do that, as they revert to one of the varieties that was bred to get the hybrid variety. The seed from GMO (genetically modified organism) plants is sterile and will not germinate.

Essential Kitchen Utensils

We've become accustomed to using all manner of small electric kitchen appliances for our cooking. Manufacturers of these devices work tirelessly to outdo each other, coming up with new things to fill our kitchen cupboards. There's one big problem though - if the power goes out, they won't work!

For that reason, it's a good idea to have manual utensils that you can use in their place. There are a lot of these available too, as people cooked long before electric appliances became available. Your needs will depend a lot on the types of things you will be cooking, but there are a few basic things you should consider:

- Manual can opener – Something you likely have. Make sure it's a good one that won't fail when trying to open all those cans.
- Tea kettle – For making coffee and tea. This should be something that can sit on an open fire.
- Hand-cranked grain mill – If you're going to stock whole grains rather than flour, you'll need to be able to grind it.
- Canning equipment – Home canning is the best way of preserving the fruit of your garden, which means having a water bath or pressure canner, as well as a can lifter and some other small utensils.
- Utensils – Speaking of utensils, the whisk is a great addition to your kitchen, allowing you to mix just about anything by hand. Make sure you have a good collection of measuring spoons and cups, as well as graters, peelers, and other hand tools for cooking from scratch.

Chapter 15
SIMPLE: First In, First Out Method

Supermarkets go through massive amounts of food every week, and it's important for them to keep that food fresh. It would be very easy for them to just keep shoving food onto the shelves, without paying attention to the expiration or best-by dates. After a while, someone would buy a can or box off the back of the shelf, take it home, and find that the product that they'd bought was expired.

Stores solve this problem by using a method called first in, first out (FIFO). As shelves are stocked, the old inventory is brought to the front and new inventory is placed behind it. What shoppers buy is actually the oldest inventory that the store has on hand, but that's not a problem because their inventory is constantly being updated.

It's a good idea to do this same with your stockpile, especially with items that are not packaged for long-term storage or items in your Tier 1 pantry (which you probably won't be repackaging). While this may not actually be necessary for some items, like canned foods, it helps ensure that your food is always fresh and not spoiled.

Create Shelf-Stable Meals

Among the many things you can do to make your meal prep easier during a time of disaster is to create shelf-stable, prepackaged meals. Some people do this in bags, others in jars, but the idea is basically the same - ingredients are put in a container together so that all it takes to prepare the meal is to boil water, add the pre-measured contents to the water, and cook.

Of course, the easiest way to go about this is to work with things that are already available as pre-packaged meals or side dishes. These can either be eaten as is or modified to make them into a more complete meal. Ideally, these should all be one-pan meals. Here are a few ideas:

- **Rice with sauce** – The flat-out fastest and easiest way of cooking rice is to buy the boil-in-a-bag variety. You can then augment that with a sauce mix in a pouch and some sort of canned meat.
- **Instant mashed potatoes** – Mashed potatoes can serve as a basis for a meal by simply adding protein.

Cook a meal-sized package of mashed potatoes, preferably one that has spices already added, then add a can of chicken or other protein.

- **Cup of noodles** – We've all seen these and probably have some in the pantry. They make a quick meal, but can also be dressed up by adding meat and/or vegetables to them.

- **Mac and cheese** – This kids' favorite can be doctored up as well. One of my favorite proteins to add is ground beef. But don't limit your thinking to only ground beef - what about canned corned beef? How about rehydrating some jerky and mixing that in?

- **Boxed soups** – Canned soups are a common quick meal, but the boxed ones work well too, plus they take up less space and will keep for years. Tomato bisque can make a good meal starter. Add a bit of basil to dress it up, and then fix something to go with it. Tomato soup and tuna salad, for example, make a great meal.

All of the above shelf-stable meals depend on using pre-packaged foods, which there's nothing wrong with. But we need to realize that when we buy pre-packaged foods, we're paying someone else to mix ingredients together. For the most part, we can save money by mixing those ingredients ourselves. Considering the fact that we're talking about stockpiling a lot of food, every penny we save is important.

With canning jars, it's easy to pre-package your own meals. The idea is to put all the ingredients needed to make a one-pan meal into a jar, so all that's needed is to dump the contents of the jar into boiling water and mix it up while it cooks.

To make this work, the ingredients must be dry ones, which can be a bit challenging when you want to do something like pasta with spaghetti sauce. But if you use powdered tomato soup mix and add your own Italian seasoning, dry diced onion, and powdered garlic, you've got a dry spaghetti sauce. Add some pasta or rice for carbohydrates and some freeze-dried meat or TVP for protein, and you've got a complete meal.

The possibilities are endless, and these types of meals can be very filling and satisfying. Dehydrating your own vegetables gives you a lot to work with as well. Vegetables dehydrate easily, and many will fully rehydrate in hot water in order to make a vegetable soup out of all dehydrated veggies.

Chapter 16
STUPID (Not You, Them)

As with anything else, it's easy to make mistakes in building up your food stockpile. Many people start with good intentions, then get frustrated with the mistakes they make along the way. Some of these might actually come from listening to bad advice, while others come from not receiving any advice at all.

Fortunately, the prepping community has grown through the years, allowing us to share information with each other. Those of us who have walked the path before can write books like this one to guide those who are joining our ranks. Here are some of the top mistakes I've encountered over the years:

Storing Staples in Original Bags

As I've already mentioned, the dry foods bought in the grocery store aren't packaged for long-term storage. These foods are meant to be eaten within 3 months, and their packaging is designed as such. While many will last longer than 3 months, it can't be guaranteed without repackaging them.

The system I mentioned earlier, using aluminized mylar bags to store dry foods, is the simplest way to DIY long-term food storage. There is also the option of using a vacuum sealer, but this is not recommended because bags can leak air, which contaminates food.

Some people use another method known as "dry canning." Canning, as a means of preserving food, is intended for wet foods, and is done in a hot water bath. Dry canning is the practice of putting dry foods in cans and then putting it into the oven to heat. This accomplishes the same goal of killing off any bacteria in the food, just as long as the food reaches a minimum internal temperature of 158°F. As the jar cools, the lid seals, keeping the now sterilized food safe from bacteria and other pests.

Buying Foods Your Family Doesn't Like

Many prepping stockpile lists contain things that many people wouldn't eat unless we were really desperate. The same could be said of some of the commercially produced "survival foods" out there. It makes no sense at all to build a stockpile of food that your family is not going to eat.

But there's got to be some balance in this as well. Most of the shelf-stable foods that we can stockpile simply aren't going to taste as good as fresh foods taste. It doesn't matter how much effort they put into it - canned veggies just don't taste like fresh ones.

Therefore, I recommend doing some experimental cooking and preparing of "survival foods" of your own creation for your family to try and then modifying the recipes as needed. That way, you can find out what will work and what won't. The proper use of spices often makes the difference between something your family turns their noses up at and them asking for more.

Lack of Variety

Most of us are used to eating quite a variety of different foods. We like to taste different flavors. That becomes a challenge when you're trying to work with shelf-stable foods. Something about preserving food, especially canning it, tends to take flavor away.

One solution for this is to stock a lot of variety. If you're going to stock beans, don't just stock one kind; get as many different kinds as you think your family will eat. The same can be said for grains to bake bread with. Yes, we're all used to wheat flour, but adding in a bit of barley flour or rye flour can give your family a new taste to try without it being so different that they reject it.

Bulk Buying Without Trying First

The goal is to build a stockpile that includes a lot of food. One of the common ways of doing that is buying in bulk. Just be sure that your family will eat what you're going to buy *before* investing in 100 pounds of it. Buy a 1-pound package and experiment, making a few different things out of it. If that works out, then you can buy it in bulk.

Buying Food You Don't Know How to Cook

While you'll probably end up choosing some foods you've never cooked before, you don't want to fill your entire pantry with them. You'll want to take the time to learn how to cook with these mystery ingredients before you need them.

There are a few culinary skills that any prepper should learn, including baking bread and various food preservation techniques. Learn how to gauge the quantity of food in packages, especially canned foods. Ideally, you want to use whole cans in a recipe or be able to split a can between two days to avoid waste. That's going to take some creativity in modifying recipes. I like to remember this through a quote from

Dorothy Parker: "Creativity is a combination of a wild mind and a disciplined eye."

Storing Food in Your Attic or Garage

Attics and garages are two of the worst possible places to store food. Both of these spaces suffer from the same problems – temperature and humidity fluctuations. These two conditions combine to create the perfect recipe for rancid food. Find places in your home which are protected by your home's HVAC system to keep the temperature and humidity within a reasonable range.

Stockpiling Potatoes

For some reason, a lot of people like to store potatoes. The problem is that potatoes don't store well for very long. You can store them for a few months if you happen to have a root cellar, but if you don't, their shelf life is limited. You're much better off stocking dried potatoes. They take up less space, are lightweight and easy to work with, and will last a long time.

Using the Internet to Cook

In a disaster, you may not be able to rely on the internet to look up the latest and greatest recipes. You'll need to plan ahead of time by either buying a few classic cookbooks or printing recipes to make your own.

There was a time when every new bride received *The Joy of Cooking* or *Better Homes and Gardens New Cookbook* as a wedding gift. These older cookbooks teach the basics, like how to cook eggs or debone a fish, and they also have canning and other food preservation information. They are invaluable culinary resources in a prepper's kitchen.

With a little practice, you can come up with some really unique and marvelous things for your family to eat. This skill can be invaluable when you're working with a limited pantry or working with ingredients your family isn't used to eating.

Conclusion

Food is an incredibly important part of your family's survival plan - not just to nourish your body, but also to maintain morale. When you eat well, you feel well, both physically and emotionally. If faced with a worst-case scenario event, it will give you peace of mind knowing you are prepared with a stocked pantry of nutritious ingredients to get you and your family through even the toughest of times.

There was a mess sergeant (head of an Army kitchen) in the Gulf War who oversaw the dining facility in a rear area where soldiers were sent to rest and recuperate, giving them a break from the war. His mess hall became known for the quality of their food and how much the soldiers enjoyed visiting there - not a common thing in the Army. When asked, he told reporters, "I'm in charge of morale." He saw feeding the troops as much more than just filling their bellies; rather, he was ensuring that they were able to maintain a healthy mental attitude.

This is the way that feeding our families should be approached in a time of crisis. There will be enough bad stuff going on that, although feeding your people may become challenging, it can be a simple way to make them feel good.

System #5 - WIG: Water, Industrial Bulk Food, Gear

Stockpiling Guide for Practical Home Storage Items

"The revelation to produce and store food may be as essential to our temporal welfare today as boarding the ark was to the people in the days of Noah."

— Ezra Taft Benson, former U.S. Secretary of Agriculture

Stockpiling doesn't stop with food, although food is where it usually begins. There are other things that we need to have if we're going to survive. Our greatest survival needs are generally summarized as:

1. Maintaining core body temperature – We can only survive about 30 minutes if we lose our core body heat.
2. Clean water – We can only live for about 3 days without water.
3. Food – We can only live (and function well enough to ensure our survival) for about 30 days without food

In preparing for a disaster which would put us into survival mode, food gathering is important. But it is only the bronze medal winner on the podium for staying alive longer in a survival situation. As our top 3 above clearly shows, it is crucial to have gear to help maintain your core body temperature and a repetitive source for clean water.

Chapter 17
WATER: Hydrate or Die

Ask anyone in the prepping and survival community, the Red Cross, or even FEMA, and they'll tell you that the average adult needs around 1 gallon of clean water per person per day to survive. FEMA further breaks that down to 0.5 gallon for drinking, 0.25 gallon for cooking, and 0.25 gallon for cleaning.

A person can live about a week without *any* water, but only under ideal conditions. Factors such as exertion, health, and age will cause your body to lose water faster. Many sources say that a human could live 7 to 14 days with only about 16 ounces of water consumed per day. Increase that daily consumption to 34 ounces, and one could live for about 30 days.

The optimum daily fluid intake is 125 ounces for an adult male and 90 ounces for an adult female. A popular health recommendation, commonly known as the "8x8" rule, has you drinking eight 8-ounce glasses of water per day. Again, there are multiple factors that play into this calculation, and when discussing emergency preparedness and disasters you must consider manual labor, which in turn will cause your body to sweat. Assuming you're in a survival situation, you're likely doing physical labor that will make you perspire, especially if you're living in a hot climate where your body can sweat out more than 1 gallon of water per day. In a case like that, you'll likely need 2 to 3 gallons of water per person per day.

How Much Water?

Using the bare minimum figure of 1 gallon of water per person per day, a family of four will need 120 gallons of water to survive for 30 days. This water will be used for drinking, cleaning, and cooking.

Storing this amount of water can feel unattainable, so it's important to remember that having proper filtration devices counts toward your water storage numbers as well - part of your 120 gallons of water can be sourced from the creek down the road, your rain barrels, or a well if necessary. If you do want to store 120 or more gallons of water in your basement, you should feel that it's affordable, accessible, and easy to store.

As you increase your stored water volume, keep in mind that it will take more effort, both financially and in regard to the space needed to store large quantities of water. Consider these variables when deciding how you'll keep clean water stored for your family, how much water you'll keep, and what filtration and purification methods you'll use and need to have on hand.

This bears repeating - you MUST have multiple options for sourcing, capturing, filtering, purifying, and storing water. You cannot rely on only stored water or only filtration.

Stored Water Containers

The bigger problem for many people isn't the space stored water takes up; it's what type of container to use for storing that water. As a general rule of thumb, larger containers make for more efficient water storage. Only utilize smaller containers for places where you can't fit large ones, such as under the bed.

There are a lot of excellent options for water storage containers, including a number which have been designed with the idea of fitting the most amount of water in the least amount of space, just for the prepping market. Legacy Premium's 5-gallon containers are easier to work with, stack well, and hold enough water so that you're not grabbing a new water container every 5 minutes.

Home improvement stores carry 55-gallon barrels ranging from $50 to $200. These barrels are often stackable, and if you start with just 2 to 3 barrels, they can stay on the basement floor so you can easily access them in an emergency situation. Keep in mind, if you are tight with square footage, some of the larger barrels can be space hogs. Plan for storage space before bringing several 55-gallon barrels into your home.

Many of the ideal water storage containers are colored, rather than clear or white, as it helps block out sunlight, which inhibits the growth of algae. Even so, you should fill your water containers with the cleanest, purest water you can. Don't just use rainwater or tap water; either buy purified water or run your tap water through your water purification system before storing it. Bacteria and other microscopic pathogens in water can multiply in storage if the water isn't pure.

You can add a small amount of chlorine bleach to the water before sealing it up - all you need is 8 drops of bleach per gallon of water to ensure that it stays clean. If the smell bothers you, leave the container sitting open overnight after you open it and before using the water. The chlorine will evaporate, leaving behind the clean water.

Renewable Water Sources

Any water you store, as well as water that exists in your home, such as that in your hot water heater, should be looked at as your last-ditch water supply. If you're in a situation where your municipal water is down for more than a day, you don't want to work out of your water stockpile; rather, you'll want to work out of any renewable water sources that you have available to you. Save the stored water for times when you don't have anything else to use.

What do I mean by renewable water sources? Take the time to get to know the area around your home, looking specifically for lakes, ponds, canals, rivers, and streams. A lot of people have such things within 10 blocks of their homes, and all are excellent emergency water sources. Note them on a map of your own creation, showing the best route to get there, as well as good access points to get to the water.

Make sure that you have a way to collect that water, containers to put it in, and a way to get that water back to your home without having to use your car, as there may not be gasoline available. All you need is a simple cart or a child's wagon for this. Collecting the water may be the biggest hurdle, especially if the water is below street level. Working from a bridge, you might need to use something like a bucket and rope to get the water.

Well

If you happen to have a well on your property, you're truly blessed. Having a good well is the most secure water source available. Commercially drilled wells must deliver 5 gallons of water per minute to meet code. However, keep in mind that a loss of power will mean that your well pump won't work. Make sure that you either have an alternate source of power for your well pump, such as solar power or a generator, or that you have a manual pump that you can install down in the well casing to pump water by hand. Test your backup system to make sure it works.

Rainwater Capture

For those who don't have a well, rainwater capture is an excellent option and is a whole lot cheaper than putting in a well. If your home already has gutters and downspouts on it, then you've got half the system in place. All you need to do is add rain barrels to capture and store the water.

Rain barrels should be installed up off the ground on a stand so that you can use a spigot to get water from the barrels. It's a good idea to gang multiple barrels together so that you can capture and store more water. If one rain barrel holding 50 gallons of water is good, then three rain barrels holding 150 gallons is better. All it takes is some PVC pipe and fittings to gang the tanks together.

If you live in an arid part of the county, rainwater capture will probably still be worth your while, as you will get some rain. When it rains in those arid places, it tends to rain hard. That's when you need those rain barrels ganged together, giving you an opportunity to harvest as much water as possible.

Water Purification

All water harvested from nature is suspect. There's a very high likelihood that the water will be filled with microscopic pathogens (disease-causing microbes, bacteria, and more) that can cause severe illness and even death. You can't see these pathogens, so you can't trust that the water is clean just because it looks clear.

There are a lot of different methods of purifying water; I'm just going to cover some of the most effective and easy to work with ones for survival.

Filtration

Filtration is the most common means of making water safe to drink, but not all filtration systems will purify water. Many are intended to do no more than remove sediment and make the water clear. Many faucet and whole-house systems fall into this category. If the system doesn't say "removes 99.99% of bacteria" somewhere on the package or in the product information, don't buy it.

The best water filtration system on the market is the Berkey system. While expensive, the Berkey filter cartridges will filter up to 3,000 gallons of water each, making them considerably cheaper to use per gallon than anything else out there.

Another excellent filter to own is the Lifestraw. Originally developed for use in third-world countries where they often don't have clean water, the Lifestraw is a straw-type personal filtration system, allowing you to drink directly from any body of water when you're away from home.

If you're harvesting your own water all the time, such as from a well, you should also consider a reverse osmosis system. This isn't actually a filter system, as it uses a semi-permeable membrane to filter the water. About one-third of the water run through the system is discharged down the drain as "effluent" and can't be considered potable water. However, that water can still be used as "gray water" to water your garden or for cleaning (bathing, washing clothes, and cleaning your home).

Chemical Purification

Ordinary tap water normally passes through two types of purification: filtration and chemical purification. Chemical purification alone doesn't remove sediment, although it will make the water safe to drink. The chemical most often used is chlorine, which is the same thing used in swimming pools.

This can be bought as pool chemicals or in the form of chlorine bleach for washing clothes.

If you use chlorine bleach for water purification, make sure that you buy the unscented kind and avoid the "color safe" bleach, as it isn't chlorine. It takes 8 drops of normal bleach per gallon of water to purify it. Just add the bleach, stir it in, and give it about 20 minutes to work. For larger containers, you should use 20 drops per cubic centimeter - you can use a graduated cylinder to measure out the bleach.

Pool shock can also be used in place of bleach. It's a different form of chlorine – calcium hypochlorite. To use it, dilute one teaspoon of the powder in a gallon of water. Then, use 2/3 ounce (20 milliliters) per gallon of water, mixing it in and allowing it time to sit, as with the bleach.

Heat Purification

Heat purification is unique in that it can be done with ordinary things that people have in their kitchens. The basic idea is to boil the water, which will kill any pathogens and make the water safe to drink; however, it will not remove sediment. If you don't have a filter to use, most sediment will settle to the bottom of the container if you leave the water sitting overnight, and then you can pour off the clear water to use.

You don't have to bring water all the way to its boiling point to purify it, as most of the pathogens that concern us will die at 158°F. Heating the water to this point and holding it there for a few minutes is sufficient. This process is called "pasteurization." It saves fuel by not requiring the water to be heated as much.

In order to pasteurize water, you're going to need some way to determine its temperature. This can be done with a normal kitchen thermometer, like the digital ones used for checking meat. A WAPI (water pasteurization indicator) is useful as well. This is a reusable device that was developed for use in third-world countries. The WAPI consists of a wax bead inside a plastic capsule. it will melt at 160°F, indicating that the water is pasteurized.

Chapter 18
INDUSTRIAL BULK FOOD

One of the best ways of buying food for your stockpile is buying in bulk, which allows you to save a considerable amount of money on your stockpile. Since you're going to be building a stockpile of a large quantity of food, it only makes sense to get it for the best possible price. Buying in bulk from the warehouse stores is one great option, but you can also buy bulk food from restaurant supply companies. Another good option are the Amish and Mennonite stores if you have one in your area. They buy wholesale and pass the food on, repackaged, for little to no profit.

Not all foods can be purchased in bulk, but a few of the best to add to your stockpile include:

- Pasta
- Canned meats

- Powdered eggs
- Cheese encased in wax - if it's properly encased in wax, it will last for years without refrigeration
- Protein bars
- Drink mixes
- Peanut butter
- Salt
- Honey
- Sugar
- Condiments - most are vinegar based, so they'll last for years
- Beans/legumes
- Whole wheat flour - preferably whole grains that you can grind yourself
- Potato flakes
- Oatmeal
- Popcorn
- Pilot crackers - a modern day version of hardtack

The average adult eats about a ton of food per year. That's a lot of food that you're eventually going to have to buy, repackage, and store. It may be a bigger outlay of cash to purchase larger packages, but ultimately it will save money.

Don't worry - you don't have to take out a second mortgage to buy all that food at once. Nobody does that. Rather, a stockpile should be built up gradually over time. Start by trying to get a month's worth of food stored up, then add to that, a month at a time, until you reach your ultimate goal.

Don't be rigid about that though; be flexible and make exceptions so that you can take advantage of bulk purchases and sales.

The following list is to give you an idea of just how much food the average adult goes through in 90 days. There are other such lists around that reflect the ideas of different preppers. Don't take it as a hard and fast rule, as your personal cooking and eating habits may very well be different, but it can serve to give you an idea of just how much food you need. Some things, like meats, are missing, as this list was created to be a budget list, rather than a "what I'd like to eat" list.

- Wheat - 75 pounds
- Rice - 25 pounds
- Oat/grain - 25 pounds
- Pasta - 5 pounds
- Boxed potatoes - 10 pounds
- Beans/lentils (dry) - 5 pounds.
- Canned fruit - 20 pounds
- Canned veggies - 5 pounds
- Powdered eggs - 1 pound
- Canned meat - 10 pounds
- Dried milk - 10 pounds
- Peanut butter - 4 pounds
- Salt - 2 pounds
- Oils - 2 quarts
- Sugar - 10 pounds

Food Preservation

Obviously, most of the food that you're going to buy for your stockpile is going to be preserved in some way, preferably without chemicals. Most of the food preservation methods that we use have been around for centuries, so rest easy knowing that these are proven methods if they are done correctly.

For the purpose of survival, you want to avoid using refrigeration or freezing. It's not uncommon for the power to go out in a disaster, and your cold stuff would quickly spoil unless eaten right away or you find an alternate source of power like a generator.

Dehydrated Foods

Anyone who has eaten beef jerky is familiar with dehydrated food. Jerky was a staple for Native Americans, who dried their meat by placing it over poles in the sun. A lot of food we buy is dehydrated, including dried beans and pasta, but when we talk about dehydrated foods, we're typically talking about meats, vegetables, and fruit.

In the modern era, people mostly use electric dehydrators, and two of the best brands on the market are made by Excalibur and Nesco. You can buy cheaper dehydrators, but they don't have the same functionality. The big advantage of these brands is that they have a fan in them, which pushes the heated air all the way through the cabinet, ensuring that everything dries at the same rate. Lower-cost dehydrators do not have this.

The reason why dehydration works as a food preservation method is that bacteria need a moist environment to survive. By removing moisture from the food, any bacteria are killed, and invading bacteria cannot survive. Many dehydrated foods, like jerky, are soaked in a marinade first, allowing salt to impregnate the meat, which makes it an even more hostile environment for bacteria.

Keep in mind that not all food dehydrates well. It's generally not recommended to dehydrate high-fat, high-protein foods, such as olives, avocadoes, or nuts.

Freeze-Drying

Freeze-drying is similar to dehydrating, as it also preserves food by removing moisture. However, the methodology is quite different. Freeze-drying changes the texture of the dried foods, making it possible for freeze drying to work for some foods that don't dehydrate well, like avocados.

The freeze-drying process consists of dropping the temperature of the food to -40°F and then subjecting it to a strong vacuum, drawing off the now-frozen water. The resulting food will have a better texture and flavor than dehydrated and can last for up to 30 years when stored with a desiccant.

The drawback to freeze-drying is that the equipment is very expensive, putting it outside the reach of most preppers. However, that doesn't stop us from buying freeze-dried foods, which are available from most of the companies who provide commercially packaged survival food. Legacy, Mountain House, Augason Farms, and Thrive all produce a variety of freeze-dried foods.

Canning

Another important food preservation method in use today is canning. At least one complete aisle in the grocery store is filled with canned foods, including canned meats, vegetables, and fruit. You can also find canned meals, such as soups, stews, and other prepared foods. A variety of foods that people tend to use rather regularly, like spaghetti sauce and applesauce, are also canned.

Although canned foods will have a best-by date stamped on them, that doesn't mean that those foods have to be used by that date. As long as the can has not lost its integrity and the lid is still concave, the food inside is still good. Canned foods up to 80 years old have been opened and found to be perfectly edible. The one exception is canned foods in plastic jars; air can still seep through the plastic, allowing the food to spoil.

Many preppers do their own canning at home, especially if they have an extensive vegetable garden. The best canned foods are always those which have been canned when they are at their peak freshness, so you can get better canned foods by canning your own.

The canning process is fairly simple. Food is cleaned and cut, then packed in canning jars and covered with either salt-water or, in the case of fruit, sugar water. The lid and ring are placed loosely on the jar, and it is immersed in a hot water bath for a specified amount of time, allowing the contents to come to a temperature high enough to pasteurize the food. The jars are then removed from the bath. As the contents cool, a vacuum is created, pulling the jar's lid down to seal.

You should always use a recipe for canning, as they will provide the necessary details about times and temperatures, as well as any necessary ingredients in the water that's put in the jar. The USDA did extensive testing on this in the last century, and all canning recipe books are based on that research. More information is available on their website. Make sure that everything you use in the canning process is sterilized to reduce the risk of contamination.

Pickling

Many people think of pickling as a part of canning, mostly because pickled foods are usually canned as well. However, the pickling process actually changes the food that is being pickled. For many foods, this is because vinegar is used in the pickling process, and the acid in the vinegar kills the bacteria that is naturally found in the food.

Both fruits and vegetables can be pickled, but not all fruits and vegetables pickle equally well. Bell peppers (of any color), green beans, cucumbers, cabbage, carrots, cauliflower, beets, wild leeks, green chili peppers, and eggplant are examples of vegetables that pickle well. As for fruit, some of the best to pickle are mangoes, apples, pineapples, and lemons.

As with canning, you should always work with a recipe for pickling to ensure that you are using the right quantities of the right ingredients to get the desired results.

Chapter 19
GEAR

In many cases, you'll be using the same gear that you use every day, especially if you are bugging in. However, there will be some special things you're going to need. Some of these are covered in the appropriate sections of this book, but there is also a need for some basic survival tools. While most people think of these things as wilderness survival gear, you'll find yourself using them at home as well.

Before digging into specific gear, there are a couple of important things to note. First, as the prepping market has grown, many companies have come out with various survival gadgets, marketing them directly towards preppers. This is a good thing, as it has given preppers many more options to pick from. At the same time, there's a lot of gear on the market that is gimmicky and not useful. It's easy to get fooled by advertising for the latest piece of gear that you "just have to have." Unless you can see a real use for it that can't be met with what you already have, you probably don't need it.

The second thing to consider is quality. This is gear that you're going to be depending on for your very survival. As such, you don't want to go cheap. Generally speaking, cheap gear is likely to fail when you need it the most. That's not to say that all expensive gear is great - some is certainly over-priced. But by avoiding the cheap stuff, you at least avoid equipment that's likely to break.

There's a saying in the prepping community that "Two is one and one is none." Anything can break, even high-quality gear, so you want a secondary way of meeting that need if a critical piece of gear breaks. Your secondary piece of equipment doesn't have to be quite as high-quality; it just needs to be serviceable.

Knives

A good knife is the most important piece of survival gear you can own. Bear Grylls, one of the better-known survival instructors, is quoted as saying, "A knifeless man is a lifeless man." In a survival situation, there are literally hundreds of ways a knife can be used, even taking the place of other tools you might carry. But if you don't have a knife, then you're likely to not be able to do some critical tasks.

Picking a knife is a very personal thing. You've got to figure out what works best for you, which might take buying and using a variety of knives until you settle on a favorite. There are a lot of people out there, myself included, who have a bunch of different knives they've bought, used for a period of time, and then set aside, finding them lacking in some way.

Some of the things to consider when looking at knives:

- **Steel quality** – A knife is all about the steel. Most knives today are made of some variety of stainless steel. There are many different grades used, and some are better than others. Stainless steel is great in that it doesn't rust, but stainless steel doesn't hold an edge as well as high-carbon steel does.
- **Fixed or folding blade** – Your main survival knife should have a fixed blade. Folding knives are a convenience, but they can break when subject to the stresses of some survival tasks. Carry a folding-blade knife for everyday use, but get a good fixed-blade knife for survival.
- **Tang** – The tang of a knife is the part of the blade that extends up through the handle. There are full-tang, partial-tang, and no-tang knives out there. You definitely want a full-tang knife, as anything else is likely to break at the most inopportune moment.
- **Blade shape** – There are a variety of different blade shapes available, each with its pros and cons. This is

one of those areas where you'll want to experiment with some different knives and find what works best for you.

- **Serrated blades** – Partially serrated blades have become extremely popular, especially for folding knives. The serrating makes it easier to cut certain things, like wet rope, but it can also make it harder to use the knife for other purposes.
- **Sheath** – Be sure to buy a knife with a good sheath which will protect the blade and protect you from harm.

I personally like the KA-BAR TD. KA-BAR knives were originally developed for the US Marine Corps and have a long and honorable history. They are well-made knives, made from quality steel with no frills. However, KA-BAR is not the only good brand out there. I have a friend who is a big fan of Gerber knives, saying that they are a good value for the money.

One thing to watch out for are gimmick "survival knives." These will often have a ferro rod mounted to the sheath, match storage compartment in the handle, or other "survival" additions. I've even seen one that has a sheath that can be used as a slingshot. To cover the cost of these add-ons, the manufacturer cuts back on the quality of the materials used for the rest of the knife, especially the steel, ultimately causing you to lose more than you gain.

Woodcutting Tools

Another big area of gear is woodcutting tools, including saws, hatchets, axes, and even machetes. Wood is a renewable resource and one of the few resources that we can harvest ourselves with minimal equipment. In a survival situation, wood can be used for building shelter, making repairs, heating, cooking, and even making weapons.

Again, there are a lot of choices available to us, enough that it would take a long time to talk about them all. Different people will find that different things work well for them, so it's imperative that you determine your own needs and preferences and choose tools based on that information. You need to be able to do two things with wood: cut it and split it. Split wood burns much better than wood that isn't split because one of the things that bark does is protect the wood within from fire. Splitting wood requires a hatchet, a maul, or a splitting wedge and hammer. What you decide to use will depend on where you are located.

Axes and mauls are different in that the ax has a thin blade that is designed to penetrate the side of a tree, across the grain, for felling a tree. A maul, on the other hand, has a much thicker blade because it is designed to go into the end grain, separating the grain so that the wood splits. Therefore, any hatchet that isn't thick enough to split wood is going to be ineffective. Likewise, tomahawks, which some people have started to use instead of hatchets, are going to be ineffective for splitting wood. They're a weapon, not a woodcutting tool.

Hatchets and axes aren't used for cutting logs to length; that's the work of a saw. Ideally, you need a saw with large teeth so that it can cut quickly. The best saws for this job are bow saws or bucking saws.

However, these saws aren't very practical for carrying in a pack. Out in the woods, you need something lightweight and compact. Manual chain saws are popular for this, but a better option is a folding pruning saw.

Flashlights

A good flashlight is an essential piece of survival gear, as well as a useful tool to have around at any time. Today's tactical flashlights, with high-intensity LEDs, are a huge improvement over the flashlights of a generation ago. They are much brighter, more compact, and don't break when they are dropped.

One thing you need to be sure of with these tactical flashlights is that you have plenty of batteries. The brighter ones can be energy hogs. I'd recommend rechargeable batteries with a good solar charger.

You also might want to consider buying an LED headlamp. Wearing a headlamp allows you to have both hands free, making it easier to work on a wide variety of tasks. The wide-angle headlamps are easier to use, shining an arc of light over a larger area; but keep in mind that, because the light is spread out, it won't be as bright.

Communications

One of the easier things to overlook in the gear department is communications. We're all so accustomed to using our cell phones that we don't always think of what we would use if the cell phone system went out. Plus, if the power goes out, you might have a problem charging your phone.

Start with a good solar charger for your phone. Make sure that it is one that provides ample current. The ones that fit in your pocket don't fit the bill even though they are advertised to be phone chargers. You're going to need a larger one, like the folding solar chargers, or you're only going to be able to use your phone one day out of every three or four.

Some sort of radio for hearing the news is essential. A hand-crank radio is a great option because it doesn't require batteries. You can even find hand-crank radios that will pick up the amateur radio bands. This will allow you to pick up ham radio operators if the local radio stations are down. For the last 100 years or more, the amateur radio network has served as a backup for government and military communications.

Finally, it can be helpful to have some sort of two-way radios so that you can keep in touch with your family while working. Business-type radios tend to have more range than civilian ones, making them a better option.

Don't Forget the 5 Bs

Stockpiling in an emergency is an extensive operation, requiring much more than food and water. The "5 Bs" are necessary items that people tend to forget: blankets, bullets, books, booze, and board games.

Blankets – When the electricity goes out, so does the heating in your home. Extra blankets are essential for keeping family members warm, especially while they sleep. You can't have too many.

Bullets – Historically speaking, the criminal element turns out in droves during the aftermath of any crisis, looting and taking advantage of people. If the food situation becomes bad enough, those same people may very well be breaking into homes, holding people up for their food. You may need to be ready to defend your family from such an attack.

Books – Don't rely on the internet for survival. It's a great resource now, but it won't do you any good if the power goes out. At that time, you're going to need printed books that contain all the information you need. This includes basic survival information, plant identification for edible plants, medical information, recipes, and a whole lot more - not to mention the fact that novels can also provide hours upon hours of entertainment.

Booze – Okay, you *can* survive without it, but does that mean you should? Alcohol has many uses beyond consumption, including using it to clean out wounds. It is also one of the best bartering supplies you could possibly have.

Board Games – Again, you can survive without them if you're willing to take the risk of your family coming down with cabin fever. You are all going to need some sort of diversion, and board games don't require the internet or electricity. They provide cheap entertainment that will last.

For more gear information and checklists, go to www.lighthousesurvival.net/bonus.

Conclusion

Clean water is critical to your family's survival. Making sure that you have water sources available that you can turn into clean, drinkable water is critical. Don't just depend on one source or one method of water purification. Have backups to make sure that you will never run out.

Expanding your stockpile is a constant, ongoing proposition. It's also important to not only have the equipment, but to do occasional preventative maintenance checks to make sure that everything is in good working condition. There are always other things that we "need" and can find to buy. Take care in making those additions though, whether they are supplies or gear. While you want to have everything you need, you don't want to get caught in the trap of buying things just because someone else says you need them.

As you add more gear to your arsenal, make sure that you work with it, learning how to use each item effectively. The middle of a winter blizzard isn't the time to learn how to split wood. You're much better off learning that skill when you don't actually need the wood. The same can be said for just about any piece of survival gear you'll own. As Murphy's Law states, **if anything can go wrong, it will**. Even the most thoughtful checklists and robust equipment need backups.

System #6 - GROW: Goals, Research, Options, Work

GARDEN Off-Grid to Feed Your Family

"The glory of gardening: hands in the dirt, head in the sun, heart with nature. To nurture a garden is to feed not just on the body, but the soul."

— Alfred Austin

No matter how big your food stockpile is, you'll eventually run out of food if you're faced with a big enough disaster. While such incidents are extremely rare, if one should happen, you're going to need some way of feeding your family over and above what you have stockpiled. Gardening is a great way to meet that need. It can also be used to stretch your food supply so that it doesn't run out in an emergency.

There are many other reasons besides survival to grow your own food, including having better tasting, fresher produce to eat; wanting to avoid pesticides and GMOs; and wanting your family to get the maximum possible nutrition out of the food you eat. Gardening provides all of these advantages and more, while also ensuring that you have a backup food supply for emergencies.

There's something rather amazing about gardening - putting a seed in the ground and then seeing a plant sprout up, grow, and give you healthy food that you can eat. There's a tremendous sense of satisfaction in the process - by investing just a little bit of time and effort each day, you're rewarded with a tangible bounty of food to feed your family.

Gardening provides other advantages as well, such as giving you a great way to relax after a hard day of work. Many people find growing things to be therapeutic, putting them back in touch with nature. That alone can make your life easier, even though it may seem like you're taking on more work.

Chapter 20
GOALS of Your Garden

Before grabbing a shovel and starting to dig, it would be a good idea to sit down and think about what you're expecting to get out of your garden. People start gardens all the time without any specific goals. Then, when things don't go as expected, they get discouraged and quit. You will have problems and get frustrated - that's one of the biggest reasons you need a goal.

So, what is your goal? Why are you thinking about growing your own food instead of taking the easy route and buying it in your local supermarket? Growing your own food:

- Provides an alternate food source that stretches your food stockpile
- Allows canning of your own food, making more personalized, better tasting canned goods

- Gives enjoyment of getting out and working with your hands and growing something
- Keeps you active and improves your physical health
- Can be a hobby to learn and then teach others
- Improves your mental well-being by putting you in touch with nature
- Teaches your children valuable life skills
- Allows you to easily avoid GMOs, pesticides, and other things that aren't healthy for you

You don't need to pick just one of these or even pick any of them. Just make sure that you understand why you're growing a vegetable garden, and remind yourself often of your reasons why.

Planning Your Garden

The first step is to determine how large your garden needs to be to feed your family. Many people are content with small, hobby-type vegetable gardens, but those won't grow enough to feed your family in the wake of a disaster.

On average, you can figure about 200 square feet of garden per family member, but that's only a rough number. A lot depends on how much space you have and what types of produce you're planning on growing, as some plants take up more space than others, which creates the need for a bigger garden. There's a great calculator for this on the Morning Chores website.

Keep in mind that this calculator doesn't account for any grains other than corn. Grains generally take up a lot of space. If you want to grow wheat, for example, you'll need about 1,000 square feet (the size of an average backyard) just to grow one bushel. A bushel is enough to yield 42 loaves of bread weighing 1-1/2 pounds each, so that 1,000 square feet wouldn't quite give you enough flour to bake one loaf of bread per week.

Of course, even 200 square feet of garden per family member would give you a good-sized garden, possibly taking up just about your entire yard. It does take a lot of work to get a garden up and running, so it's best to start small, then add to your garden each year until you reach the ideal size.

Best Garden Location

You may be limited on possible garden locations, but if you can, you'll want to select a spot in your yard that will do the most to provide your garden the things it needs to grow properly. Fortunately, plants are simple and don't have a lot of requirements. On the other hand, if any of those requirements are not met, the plants don't do well.

To start with, most plants need a lot of sunlight. This means selecting a space that naturally receives sunlight, rather than one that's shaded. Most plants won't grow as heartily in the shade, although there are a few that do. If you have no other option than to put a portion of your garden in a shady area, make sure you research which plants can tolerate less sun.

A south-facing garden is the best, as it will receive sunlight all day long. Avoid north-facing gardens in the northern hemisphere, as you're going to have more shade than sun. If you can't get that southern sunshine, then an east- or west-facing garden can still provide enough sunlight for plants to grow, with the east-facing garden receiving more sunlight in the morning and the west-facing garden receiving more sunlight in the afternoon. Adjust your watering for these hours so that you are not watering at a time when the water will evaporate quickly.

The next consideration is elevation changes. Ideally you want fairly flat land, with just enough slope to provide good drainage. Drainage is necessary so that you don't have any standing water. Too much water will kill plants just as quickly as too little. Check for puddles in your yard the next time you get a heavy rain. Are there low spots that don't drain well? If there are, you either want to avoid them or fill the low spot to eliminate it.

Not all low spots will have obvious puddles forming in them. Even so, most low spots are rather obvious, as they won't dry out as quickly as the rest of your yard. You may even see algae growing on the ground, while the plants themselves end up with yellowish, wilted leaves.

A garden on a hillside is difficult to water, as the water tends to run off too fast. The solution to this is to terrace the garden, giving yourself flat areas that you can use for planting. Make sure there is still some drainage so that the water doesn't just sit on the terraces.

Soil Quality is Critical

The most important part of any garden is the soil. In addition to being anchored in the soil, plants receive their water and nutrition from the soil. Soil that's too hard won't allow water to get to the roots of the plants, and soil that doesn't have the proper nutrients will keep the plants from growing to their full stature and, therefore, from providing an abundant harvest.

Don't expect your yard to come equipped with good soil. What you have might be good for growing grass, but that doesn't mean that the soil is good enough to grow plants in your garden. Those require much more water and nutrition.

Dig down into your soil and see what you have. How dark is it? If you can't see a lot of organic matter that is in the process of breaking down, turning it nice and black, then your soil is lacking nutrients, and may even be lacking the necessary insect life to properly break down that organic matter.

Chances are, you'll need to bring in some good soil or at least the nutrients necessary to fortify your soil and make it good for gardening. Compost or composted manure is a great way to bring in extra nutrients. You'll also want to add worms to the soil, as they are one of the main workers in the process of breaking down organic matter and returning nutrients to the soil.

Chapter 21
RESEARCH: Indoor Gardening Tools, Security for Your Prepper Garden

Not everyone lives in suburbia with a nice big backyard that can be used for gardening. We don't want to forget the 17% of our population who live in apartments. Besides, no matter how much space you have outside for gardening, chances are high that you won't be able to garden year-round. So, you might want to consider doing some indoor gardening to supplement your outdoor one.

Believe it or not, there are a wide variety of ways of growing food indoors, starting with hanging pots or container gardening on the kitchen windowsill. Did you know that you can grow strawberries upside-down out of a hanging pot? If you're going to have greenery in your home or apartment anyway, why not use dwarf fruit trees, which will give you a harvest?

Apartments with balconies provide a real advantage, as food can be grown on that balcony, especially if it is south facing. This is where the concept of vertical gardening really helps. Make racks that will hold your pots, allowing you to stack several plants in the same square foot of space. Vertical gardening can be taken indoors as well - you can build a garden right in the window.

Remember that plants need sunlight, water, air, and soil to grow, and nothing more, so be creative about how you use your space. In spaces that don't get natural light, mirrors can be used to redirect the sunlight that comes in through the windows. Daylight light bulbs exist as well, allowing you to create artificial daylight from any lamp.

Some of the best plants to grow indoors include:

- Tomatoes
- Scallions
- Garlic
- Lettuce
- Green beans
- Peas
- Strawberries

That may not give you enough for your entire diet, but it's a start. Your ability to add to that list will depend more on your *use* of available space rather than the *amount* of space you have to work with.

Microgreens

Microgreens are another great planting method to use indoors. Microgreens are the small beginnings of plants with fully formed leaves. They differ from sprouts in that sprouts are harvested before the leaves form fully. Microgreens are high in vitamins C and E, and they're a good source of beta-carotene.

There are pre-made kits available for starting microgreens, but they can be grown in any available container, even disposable containers from your restaurant leftovers. Plastic containers work better than styrofoam, as they don't break as easily. Holes need to be drilled in the bottom of the container to allow drainage, then fill them with starter soil, add the seeds, and add a little more soil to top it off.

Rather than pouring water on your microgreen garden, you'll be better off misting the soil or plants with a spray bottle. Spray whenever it seems dry, but at least once per day. The greens will grow to cutting height in 7 to 14 days, depending on the plant type. They can grow back, so don't cut them too short. Typically, you can cut microgreens several times, enjoying them for topping salads or other dishes.

Some of the best plants to use for microgreens are:

- Lettuce
- Sunflower

- Alfalfa
- Pea shoot
- Radishes
- Red cabbage
- Basil
- Kale

Protecting Your Garden

While plants don't need much in order to grow, there's plenty out there that can hinder their growth. The same plants that you are growing for food will be seen as a buffet to a wide range of critters, spread out and ready for their eating pleasure. One of your biggest challenges will be protecting your garden from them so that your family gets to enjoy what you're growing.

Insects are usually the biggest threat to any garden. There are a variety of different insects that will want to eat the fruit of your garden or the plants themselves. Some people use insecticides to control these pests, but you can do just as well by introducing beneficial insects to your garden. NaturesGoodGuys.com specializes in beneficial insects that can protect your garden.

Birds will eat insects as well. If you have chickens, allowing them to forage around your garden will do a lot to keep the insect population at bay, while providing much-needed protein for the chickens. But be careful with this, as chickens will eat just about anything - including the garden itself.

Another option is to attract wild birds to your garden by putting in a bird feeder and a bird bath. The birds will eat the birdseed but will also pick off any insects that they see. However, they eat beneficial insects too, so you need to decide what you'd prefer.

There are even plants which will work to repel some types of insects because they don't like the smell of those plants. Some good ones are basil, catnip, mint, rosemary, and citronella.

When it comes to the larger pests like squirrels, gophers, and moles, you simply must keep them out of the garden. One option is to fence in your garden, including putting some sort of roof over it that still allows sunlight to come through. Raised beds can help with burrowing pests, especially if you put poultry netting or hardware cloth in the bottom of the planting beds.

Weather can be a big issue as well. Wind, rainstorms, frost, and even sun can cause problems for your garden. You'll want to keep a close eye on the weather so that you know just how much to water or when to provide your plants with some extra protection. When that first frost comes in the fall, it's time to harvest everything you still have in the ground so that it doesn't freeze and go bad.

Chapter 22
OPTIONS: What to Plant?

S electing what to plant in your garden can be as challenging as selecting what to store in your food stockpile. While you might want to stretch your family's culinary experience slightly, you're going to be much better off sticking to foods that you know your family will eat. This is especially true in a survival situation, where the food we eat plays a major part in our morale.

The trick is to balance taste and nutrition. Granted, you're not going to be able to grow Twinkies in your garden, so you won't be able to satisfy junk food cravings. However, you do want food that your family will enjoy eating and that provides the nutrition that they need.

Not everything will grow in all areas of the country. You may be limited by the climate you live in. Apples, for example, don't grow well during the summer in the deep south because of the heat. This may seem obvious but pick plants that will thrive in the area where you live. To make it easier, the USDA has divided the country into 10 growing zones, which has proven to be a very valuable resource. Seed packets are typically labeled with their ideal growing zones, so it's just a matter of finding varieties that will grow where you are.

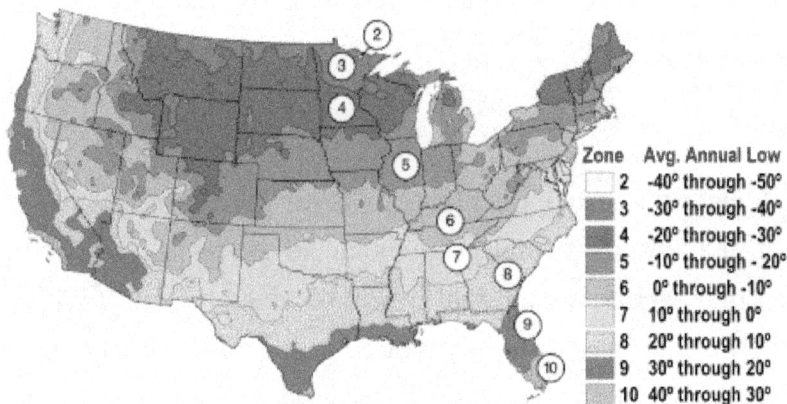

Zone	Avg. Annual Low
2	-40° through -50°
3	-30° through -40°
4	-20° through -30°
5	-10° through -20°
6	0° through -10°
7	10° through 0°
8	20° through 10°
9	30° through 20°
10	40° through 30°

Another important factor to keep in mind is that you want to plant heirloom seeds rather than planting hybrid or GMO seeds. Not only will you get better tasting produce, but the seeds from that produce can be harvested and planted next year. This might not seem like much of an issue right now, but it could become a huge one in a TEOTWAWKI scenario, when you can't just go to the garden center to buy more seeds.

Some of the best vegetables to grow in your garden are:

- Green beans
- Pinto or black beans
- Squash of various types, including zucchini
- Tomatoes
- Radishes
- Potatoes
- Romaine lettuce
- Swiss chard
- Bell peppers
- Onions
- Lentils
- Carrots
- Spinach
- Cucumbers
- Garlic
- Berries of various types

In addition, it's a good idea to grow herbs, like rosemary, basil, cilantro, parsley, dill, mint, and oregano. Herbs tend to be easy to grow, and fresh herbs have much more flavor than dried herbs. You'll eventually run out of the dried ones you stockpile, so being able to grow more just makes sense. Besides, you can always dry the herbs you grow, adding to your stockpile.

Don't Forget the Perennials

Some of the best things you can plant in your garden are perennials. These are plants that you plant once, and they come back year after year. Trees are a prime example of this, but there are several other plants that qualify. Some of the best perennials for your garden are:

- Chives
- Rhubarb
- Jerusalem artichokes
- Asparagus
- Strawberries

Don't forget fruit trees either. Since fruit trees need a few years to start producing fruit, they should be planted first, before any other part of your garden. Once they start producing, they can produce for years, providing a lot of food for your family. Keep in mind that fruit trees, like other plants, have growing zones, so choose trees that will bear fruit where you live.

Organize Your Planting Time

Most people with small gardens plant everything at the same time and hope for the best. That's not the strategy you want to adopt when growing a larger garden. If you plant everything at the same time, you'll have a massive amount of each vegetable ripening at the same time. This is a great scenario for canning, but it can be difficult for working out a menu.

Some plants will grow only one vegetable, like carrots or radishes, while others will start producing and keep producing until the first freeze of fall, like tomatoes. Start all of your tomato plants early so that you can harvest as many tomatoes as possible. On the other hand, when it comes to carrots, plant them in batches every couple of weeks, which will allow them to mature at different times.

If you live in the cooler climates in the north, you'll want to start germinating your seeds indoors or in a greenhouse, especially for plants like tomatoes, which take some time to grow. Once you have good sprouts and the weather is warm enough, transplant them outdoors to finish growing.

Chapter 23
WORK: Your Garden is a Labor of Love, but the Work is Worth It!

The greatest days in anyone's garden are harvest days. But how do you know when to pick? You want everything to reach peak ripeness before you pick it - harvesting too early or too late each creates its own issues.

Growing time can vary considerably from one vegetable to another, and each type of fruit and vegetable has its own way of telling when it is ready to harvest. Start by researching how long it typically takes for the fruit to mature.

It seems like maturity would be difficult to determine for carrots, which are a root vegetable and grow underground, but it's not so hard at all. They have a 60- to 80-day growth time. The tops of the carrots often break through the soil, allowing you to see them. Once they do that, it's a matter of waiting until they are ¾- to 1-inch in diameter with good color.

Tomatoes, a favorite in many gardens, produce from June through September, with each plant continuing to produce more tomatoes until the first frost. You can tell when the tomatoes are ready to pick because the fruit will have a vibrant color and they will pull easily from the stem.

Once picked, foods that are to be preserved should be preserved as quickly as possible to preserve their freshness.

Harvesting is hard work, but the real work actually takes place between planting and harvesting. Gardens need constant tending. It's not arduous work, but it can be time-consuming.

Watering

The general rule of thumb is that plants need about one inch of water per week, although gardens in hot climates will probably need more than that. Factor the rain into that figure as well. If it rains and that rain gives your garden at least as much as you would, then there's no need to water again.

Overwatering can be as much of a problem as underwatering, especially if you don't have good drainage. Raised beds nearly eliminate this problem, as they provide natural drainage for excess water.

You'll probably have to do some experimenting with your watering, using a meter to tell the moisture level of the soil in your garden, until you can recognize it visually or by touch. If you can pack the soil together in the palm of your hand, it's moist enough. Plants that are obviously drying up are telling you that they need more water. However, it's harder to tell when they're getting too much water, which can cause root rot and kill the plants.

It's best to water in the morning before it heats up or in the evening after the sun goes down. Avoid watering in the middle of the day, when the heat causes the water to evaporate before the plants get it.

Weeding

Weeding is a chore that many people hate, but it's not all that bad. It gives you the opportunity to enjoy time outside in your garden. Weed often when the weeds are tiny, pulling by hand or digging with a spade. The younger the weed, the shorter the root and the easier it is to remove. The bigger those weeds grow, the more water and nutrients they're going to steal from the plants you're trying to grow - and the harder they'll be to pull.

If you're new to gardening, it can be challenging to determine which plants are vegetables and which are weeds. One helpful tip is to make signs for the various things you're growing in your garden that show pictures of the plants' leaves rather than the fruit of those plants. Place them in the areas where you have planted those seeds, and as you're weeding, you'll be able to quickly reference those signs to make sure that you're pulling weeds and not food plants.

When pulling weeds, be sure to get as much of the root system as possible. It's not always easy to get every last bit of root, but if you don't, the weed will come back in a few days. I typically pull weeds by hand, although some prefer to use a weeding tool. It's fine to use what you have or what you prefer. It's best to stay away from using chemical weed killers, as those get into what you're growing and will ultimately be consumed by your family.

Maintaining

Besides watering and weeding, the most important maintenance task you have is mulching your garden. Spreading mulch over the garden will help control weeds and hold water in the soil, keeping it from drying out. Consider mulching your paths as well to keep weeds from sprouting up.

Larger, heavier plants usually require some support, like placing tomato cages over your tomato and pepper plants. Some large plants need stakes instead of cages. Vine plants grow best with a trellis, and they often need to be "trained" to grow on and around it, as they can latch onto other plants rather than staying on the trellis.

Check your garden fence regularly, looking not only for damage, but for a place which looks like something has been trying to burrow under it. A good fence is a necessary protection for any garden.

Conclusion

Gardening can be one of the most satisfying parts of your survival strategy. Should a major disaster put you in a long-term survival situation, it is that garden that guarantees your family's survival. Your stockpile will eventually run out, but hopefully your garden never will.

Gardening is such an extensive subject that entire books have been written about it. It's also something you never stop learning about. There are certified master gardeners who have been teaching others for years, but are still seeking out new things to learn themselves.

Ideally, you want to reach a point where your garden requires minimal effort. That's not the way it will seem at first, but as you get it going, it should take less and less work while providing more and more food for your family. A well-cared-for garden will produce more food each and every year.

System #7 - HOME: Heat, Outsmart, Munitions, Educate

Shelter in Place and Defend Your Disaster-Ready Turf

"There are two ways to sleep well at night: be ignorant or be prepared."

— Unknown

Up to this point, we've primarily focused on food and water - the two things that people think they need most in a survival situation. We think of food and water first because we don't need heat every day, nor do we need to defend our home from attack all the time.

The reality is that lack of heat in your home can kill you just as fast as not having food or water. Considering how easily the electrical grid can go down and that heating systems don't work without electricity; you need to be ready to keep your home warm without a functioning primary heating system. Options are limited, but there *are* options.

As for defense, I hope you'll never have to defend your home and family. But hope won't keep you safe. Even in normal times, there's a chance of your home being invaded. During a time of crisis, when people are desperate, those chances increase. The deadbolt on your door isn't going to be enough to turn away hungry people who are desperate for food.

Chapter 24
HEAT: Winter is Always Just Around the Corner

The human body is amazing in its ability to adapt to changing circumstances, especially to changing climate. We find people living in all possible climate conditions, from the hottest deserts to the frozen Arctic. But that doesn't mean that you *want* to live in those freezing conditions. We're not accustomed to it, and we really don't know what to do if our home heating goes out.

Modern forced-air heating is highly dependent on electricity. Even if your home is heated by gas, the controls and blower to move the air through the ducts still run on electricity. Without electricity, all you've got is some expensive equipment that can't be used for anything else.

Your home's insulation should keep your home livable for a day or two, even if your heat goes out. But beyond that point, you're going to have to generate some heat inside the home in order to keep your family warm. Fortunately for us, this isn't a new problem for humans, as our ancestors had to deal with it for centuries before we came along.

Heating with Wood

The most common heating system in history is woodfire. From a centrally located fire pit with a smoke hole in the roof to modern fireplaces and wood-burning stoves, mankind has had a lot of experience heating with wood. The main reason we don't use wood today is that it isn't convenient, but in a post-disaster world, wood will likely be the best heating option you can find.

Heating with wood means having either a fireplace or wood-burning stove in the home. If your home doesn't already have one, a wood-burning stove is a better option because it can radiate heat from all sides, while a fireplace is normally installed in an exterior wall and only radiates heat out the front. It's usually easier to install a wood-burning stove too, as there is no need to build something to house it in.

The biggest consideration in either case is the chimney. If you live in a single-story home, you're only going to have to run that chimney up through the attic, which isn't much of an issue. But if you live in a two-story home, the chimney has to go through the upper story as well. Few homes have space available to do that, so the space would need to be taken out of a room.

An alternative to taking that space out of a room is to run the chimney up the outside of the home. It can either be boxed in or not, based on your preference, but according to code, it must go at least 5 feet above the roof's peak.

The best, most obvious location for a wood-burning stove is your living area. If your home has a "great room" design, where the living room, dining room, and kitchen are combined into one large room, you're at an advantage - the same wood-burning stove can heat the entire area. Just be sure to buy a large enough stove for an area of that size.

But what about bedrooms? Typically, the only area that is heated by a wood-burning stove or fireplace is the main living area of the home - not the bedrooms. Putting in several fireplaces is expensive, and most bedrooms don't have enough space for a wood-burning stove anyway. This means that in an emergency where you're heating your home with wood, you're going to need to have everyone camp out in the living room until the weather warms up or the crisis passes.

Additionally, the type of firewood you use makes a significant difference in the amount of heat it produces. Dense hardwoods pack more potential energy into a log than softwoods do, so hardwood logs will burn longer and produce more heat. Even so, it's a good idea to also have some softwood, such as pine, as that's much easier to start a fire with. People who heat their homes with wood typically go through 4 to 6 full cords of wood per winter. A cord is a stack that's 4' high x 8' long x 4' deep. Some places advertise "face cords" which is much less; it's a stack that's 4' high x 8' long, but only as deep as the cut log length; usually about 16".

You can save a lot of money by advertising to cut dead trees and fallen limbs in your community. All you need is a chainsaw and something that you can haul wood in. Cutting down a tree is hard work, but it can save you a few hundred dollars.

Heating with Propane or Kerosene

Wood isn't the only option available to us if the electricity goes out. We can also heat our homes with portable propane or kerosene heaters. Both are relatively inexpensive and come in a variety of sizes, making it possible to buy a unit that will heat the amount of space you need. Propane is readily available just about anywhere, but kerosene is only found easily in the northern part of the country where people use it for space heaters. If you do live in the south and need kerosene, it can be found in paint stores; however, it's generally pretty expensive.

The limiting factor on both options is the amount of propane or kerosene you can store. Unlike wood, you can't harvest either of these fuels from nature yourself. When a crisis hits, the supply you have on hand is likely what you will have to work with for the foreseeable future, because resupplying will be a challenge. Propane and kerosene are great as short-term heating solutions, but not so good in a long-term survival situation.

Additional Ways to Heat

Historically speaking, U.S. homes' primary source for heat came from wood. Central heating became mainstream for residential use after World War II, and only became widespread starting in the 1950s. Even then, homes were not equipped with high-efficiency radiators that could heat the entire house. Luxury homes of the time may have contained this high-end feature, but it was typically the primary living space only that could be heated. To make up for this, homeowners did a variety of things. Not all are easily adaptable today, but some ideas include:

- Many homes had the sleeping area in a loft, especially for the children, so that the rising heat from the fire would keep them warm at night.
- The bedwarmer was a pan with a lid and a long arm. Rocks warmed in the coals of the fire were placed in the pan, which was then passed between the sheets, warming the bed before getting in.
- Soapstone was used for portable heat. The stone, which was usually cut into bricks, was placed in the

fire, where it could absorb heat. It was then carried in a cloth sling to wherever heat was needed. When the family drove to town in the wagon, the soapstone would be placed under the seat, warning those sitting on the seat. Anyone sitting in the back of the wagon would sit with their back to the seat so they could also receive heat from the soapstone.

- Lots of blankets on the beds. Remember great grandma's crocheting hobby? That hobby doubled as an important resource - the final product of her downtime was a durable, warm blanket or hat for those cold winters.
- Everyone dressed warmly indoors, wearing sweaters and long johns.
- Winter hats or beanies were the style back in the day, just as they are today. Wearing a winter hat kept people warm and dry and helped prevent frostbite or hypothermia. One of the easiest ways to lose body heat is from exposed skin.
- Candles and oil-burning lamps were used as hand warmers, especially when someone was doing work that required finger dexterity.
- Physical work maintains body heat. Woodcutting was normally a wintertime job, done after the crops were harvested. There would be less sap in the trees, and cutting in the winter allowed the wood to dry out and become seasoned during the spring and summer before it was needed in the fall and winter.

- Homes were kept as insulated as possible, and cracks were sealed around doors and windows to prevent drafts. Today's homes are better insulated, but care still needs to be taken to ensure minimal heat loss.
- Putting blankets or insulated curtains over the windows will help prevent heat from escaping.

Chapter 25
OUTSMART: Tips to Outwit Intruders and Fortify Your Home

As scary as it can be to think about, you have to assume that your home is going to come under attack at some time if SHTF. Desperate people tend to do desperate things. In an emergency situation where the next meal is not a given, there are few circumstances that make a person feel more helpless than seeing their kids hungry. Unless you're planning on having enough food to feed the whole community, you'd better be ready to defend what you have, as that desperation can turn to violence quickly.

Fortifying your home in both passive and active defenses is crucial. Passive defense involves the steps you take to make it harder for anyone to break into your home. Active defense refers to taking up arms in defense of your home and family. The better your passive defenses are, the less you'll need to depend on the active ones. Even then, you should also be ready to take up arms in the defense of your home.

Hardening Your Home

If we look at current statistics on home break-ins, 34% enter through the front door, while 22% enter through the back door. The next biggest entry points are ground-floor windows. If we can make those harder to get through, it will go a long way toward making your home a fortress. The first thing you want to consider is hardening your home. So what does that even mean?

Start by performing a routine security check of your home while walking through it and around the property. Home security experts often preach that you should "think like a burglar" when analyzing your personal situation. Pay attention to blindspots and certain areas that you already know need strengthening. Test all entry and exit points to your home. A home examination such as this is a wise thing to do annually, even if you are not preparing for the next catastrophe or global event.

If, for any reason, power is out for an extended period of time or there are supply chain issues regarding food, water, and gear resupplies, your home could be targeted by nefarious folks looking to steal from any place that looks like an easy target.

Is that your home? Answer these questions:

- Do you constantly leave your windows unlocked or garage doors open?
- Are there sensor lights or visible cameras on the outside of your home?
- Is there a barking dog?
- Do you know any of your neighbors well enough that you are looking out for one another from time to time?

These are just a few common home security tests to gauge where you are currently vulnerable. The goal is to arm you with some basic yet affordable ways to heighten awareness of your surroundings and improve your tactical vantage points at home.

Entry Door

It isn't hard to break in through the entry door of a home, even if there's a deadbolt installed. A swift kick near the door lock will cause most deadbolts to break through the door frame, as the wood door frame isn't strong enough to withstand blunt force. It's only ¾" thick, and the screws holding the striker plate are only ¾" long.

All it takes to defeat that swift kick is what's known as a security striker plate. There are numerous brands on the market that are effective, but you want one that's about 30"

long that's installed with screws that are at least 3" long,
filling every screw hole in the plate. Those longer screws will
go through the door frame and into the structural studs
behind them. Then, if a foot kicks the door, the force of the
kick will be spread out over a larger area and transferred by
those longer screws to the home's structure. The foot
won't win.

While you're installing that security striker plate, consider
replacing your hinges with security hinges if your front door
swings outward. The hinges of outward-swinging front
doors are exposed on the exterior of your home, allowing a
would-be intruder easy access to them. In order to break
into a house with security hinges, the bad guy would have to
pry the frame of the door away from the door itself to
remove it and gain access to the home. While you're at it,
replace the short screws with the same longer screws used to
install the security striker plate.

Back Door

If your home has a back door that's like the entry door, then
the same measures used to secure the front door will work
for the back door. However, if the door is a sliding glass
door, it's going to be harder to secure. You might want to
consider removing the sliding glass door, framing in the
opening, and putting in a standard door. If you don't want to
replace the sliding door, consider doing something to cover
it for protection.

At the very least, get a burglar bar for the sliding door, or even a wooden rod cut to length to fit within the door tracks. This is not the most secure method available, but it's one more deterrent to a desperate thief looking to gain access to your home.

Windows

The idea that locked glass windows are secure is unrealistic. All it takes to get through most windows is a rock or a hammer, as glass breaks very easily.

But glass can be made to not break quite as easily. Security window film can be installed on the inside of the window. This film, which is similar to window tinting film (but thicker and clear), holds the glass together even if it is broken. Anyone trying to break in through the window has to break the glass out all the way around, which gives you time to react as necessary.

An even more secure possibility is to install burglar bars over the windows. Fixed and adjustable burglar bars can be purchased from home improvement centers, but the best option are those that are custom-made at a welding shop. They will be made of thicker material and built to fit your windows.

Burglar bars can also be installed either on the inside or outside of the windows, but they are built for one or the other. They're more secure if they're installed on the inside, as anyone who would want to pull them off would have to pull them through the wall.

Securing Your Property

With the home itself now more secure from intruders, you can turn your attention to the property. Lights and cameras, especially the types that are motion-triggered, are an excellent deterrent against criminals in general. But if you're going to depend on them during a time of crisis, you need to make sure that you have a source of power for them, like solar or wind power connected to a battery backup system.

Pets can be useful for home defense as well. Dogs are naturally territorial and will let you know if anyone comes around. A common misconception about dogs when it comes to home defense is that they must be massize to defend your turf. Even though I have owned large dogs for years and have seen their intimidation tactics at work on unsuspecting strangers, it often seems like the smaller dogs have that early bark that will alert you sooner to potential stranger danger. These smaller pups may not charge or bite an intruder, but their built-in, early alarm system (bark-bark-bark!) can be an effective measure to buy you time if it's someone other than the Amazon driver in your driveway.

Rather than complaining about your dog's constant barking at people in the street, you *want* to have a dog that barks at them. It might bother you and your neighbors now, but your pup's bark will add security to your home in the event of a crisis.

Is your home exterior making you an easy target? Here are a few improvements to consider regarding easy-to-overlook features that can give a potential thief access to your home:

- Eliminate hiding places along fence lines or near windows that could provide a stranger enough cover to hide out until dark.
- Trim tree branches and large bushes that an assailant could shimmy up to gain access to a second-story entry point.
- Install sensor lighting near entry points along the exterior of your home that, when triggered, could scare off an intruder - the brighter, the better. Solar-powered LED lights are nice options.
- Remove any trellis systems against your home's exterior wall that a bad guy could use to easily climb to an upstairs window or door.

Many people think in terms of building a wall or a tall fence around their property to keep people out; however, you can also protect your property using landscaping as an effective security measure. Not only does this look nice, but it can deter any potential criminals who may be scoping out your neighborhood for easy targets.

Depending on which part of the country you live in, a thorny hedge is an excellent natural fence option, preferably at least 3 feet thick. If you allow it to grow to about 4 feet high, you'll have a formidable obstacle for anyone to cross.

An additional thing to consider is that your home won't stop anyone's bullets - not even if it's made from bricks - so you'll need some protection. If there is a true post-disaster situation, you might want to build a sandbag wall under a first-floor window in the front of your home. Even a 1-foot-thick wall of sandbags placed right up against the wall would provide an extra layer of protection if a gunfight happens, as drywall and brick can't stop bullets.

Those sandbags can also function as flood protection in a hurricane or any storm that may hit your home. They are affordable, versatile, and take up hardly any space when stored.

Unfortunately, if someone *really* wants to get into or attack your home, no hedge, fence, or concrete wall is going to stop them. However, applying a bit of psychology here, you can use that hedge to direct the way that people access your property, perhaps guiding them right up your front walkway. The average person will naturally take the path of least resistance, and if you leave an opening in your hedge right at the front walkway, they'll use that instead of sneaking around the sides.

Fighting Positions

This may be tough to hear, but there's a possibility that your home will come under attack during an emergency event. Desperate, hungry, and potentially armed people may attempt to harm or kill you for something you own.

It's crucial that you have a tactical positioning plan within your fortress. Even if you're a perfect shot or have years of expertise in martial arts, if three or four people break into your home, you can't defeat them on your own. It's better to deal with the invaders outside of your home, assuming you can avoid an altercation inside, but sometimes that is easier said than done.

With that reinforced front door, a solar-powered camera pointing their way, sensor lights in place, a barking dog, and a trimmed hedge that bottlenecks them, your family now has a few tactical advantages on your side if the situation escalates.

Beyond those defensive measures, you'll want to prepare yourself a fighting position in the second story, either directly above the front door or as close as possible. Remember that opening in your hedges you've strategically trimmed to point toward your front walkway? It may seem like an invitation for intruders, but it also acts as a natural pinch point. It's a lot harder to get outflanked by multiple intruders in an invasion if you have them bottlenecked into one confined area within a clear shot of your fighting position.

Height is an advantage, and if any intruders are coming up the walkway, they will be walking right into your shooting zone.

It sounds like an episode of *The Walking Dead* meets the Wild West, but as a prepper at heart, I want you to have as many advantages as possible.

Chapter 26
MUNITIONS

In a worst-case scenario event, there will probably come a time when taking up arms in defense of your home becomes a reality. Even if that extreme situation never comes to fruition, it's still important to discuss, because even the best passive home defense methods can be defeated by a determined intruder. You must be ready to defend yourself and your family with firearms.

Firearm sales were at a record high in the pandemic year of 2020, when the industry shattered previous high sales records. In 2021, the gun industry sold 19.9 million guns - about 6 guns for every 100 Americans. With these numbers, there's a good chance that you own or have considered buying at least one firearm.

There's a lot that goes into choosing a firearm. You'll need to find a gun that fits your budget, your body, and your defense needs. Everyone's style, preferences, and opinions are different - telling you which gun to choose is similar to telling you to buy a Ford rather than a Chevy. You'll need to learn the gun's proper functions, cleaning and safety, legal restraints and requirements in your area, and safe and secure storage. And, of course, you'll need lots of loading and shooting practice.

As a starting point, I'd recommend one pistol and one long gun for each shooter in your family. This is not a hard-and-fast rule, but worth considering as you prepare and plan. Pistols are great for self-defense, but once you get beyond 25 feet, it's hard to shoot them accurately. When it comes to defending your home, you'll likely be shooting further than 25 feet, so you will need a rifle or shotgun. At the same time, carrying a pistol gives you a line of defense if you don't have your long gun immediately available.

Pistols

Pistols can be broken down into two basic categories: revolvers and semi-automatic. While there are plenty of people who like revolvers, semi-automatic pistols hold more rounds in the magazine and give you the advantage of being much quicker to reload, allowing you the ability to continue shooting.

As a general rule of thumb, many people say that it's a good idea to select the largest caliber pistol that you can shoot comfortably, which means being able to shoot a box of 50 rounds without your hand feeling like it has been beat up. You also need enough strength in your hands to be able to rack the slide on the pistol, which can be a problem for some people if they have weak hands. A .380 ACP (Automatic Colt Pistol) is a good option for them, as it has little recoil and a lighter spring; however, the .380 is considered by many to be marginal as a self-defense weapon.

The other consideration is availability of ammunition. Of all the pistol calibers there are, .22LR and 9mm Parabellum, sometimes called 9mm Luger, are the most common semi-automatic rounds available. During a post-disaster time, ammunition might become scarce, so it makes sense to use a common caliber. The .22LR is a very marginal round for self-defense, so it would be better to go 9mm if you can.

9mm vs. .45 ACP

There's a big debate in the gun owners' community about whether the 9mm or the .45 ACP is the best pistol round. Both are popular, with a wide variety of gun models to choose from. The magazines for 9mm pistols generally hold more rounds because the overall size of the cartridges is smaller. On the other hand, those who prefer the .45 say it makes a bigger hole.

Both weapons were developed in the early 1900s for military use, but the actual goals behind their designs were quite different.

The U.S. Army commissioned the design of the .45 ACP because the .38 round that was used in the Army's standard sidearm wasn't powerful enough to put down Moro tribesmen who would charge their lines high on drugs. They could be hit several times and keep on coming because they didn't feel the hits. A round that was big enough and packed enough energy to knock them down was needed, so that's what the .45ACP and the Colt 1911 pistol were developed for.

On the other hand, the 9mm Luger was developed by the Germans as a general military pistol. Rather than being concerned about knocking down the target, they were concerned about hitting vital organs and either killing or seriously wounding their enemies. A pistol round which would penetrate all the way to the chest cavity, even if it had to go through an arm first, was called for, and the 9mm was designed for this. Its sharper, pointier bullet geometry and high velocity make for excellent penetration - the best of any standard pistol round on the market.

Shotguns

The shotgun, specifically the 20-gauge shotgun, has been touted by some as the ultimate home defense weapon. It has the advantage of being easy to shoot, packing a lot of punch, and having a wide variety of different types of shells available, including some not-so-lethal options. While somewhat limited in range, you should be able to shoot out to about 100 feet accurately with a shotgun, especially if it is loaded with slugs rather than shot.

Many people think of the shotgun as a point-and-shoot weapon, with the idea that the spread of the shot pattern will ensure a hit. This can be a dangerous way to think, as the amount of spread you'll get in 25 yards or less is minimal. Also, you don't want to take the chance of missing your target and hitting someone or something behind it. You must aim with a shotgun just like with any other gun.

Shotguns intended for hunting and those appropriate for home defense aren't the same. Those for home defense are the same as those used by the police. They have shorter barrels and larger magazines. You can even get shotguns that have replaceable magazines just like a pistol or rifle.

Rifles

Rifles come in a wide variety of calibers and styles. A big issue with using them for home defense is that they're considered to be overly powerful. A rifle bullet is designed to kill at a couple hundred yards, which is something that you're not going to have to do when defending your home. This isn't sniper warfare - if you try to kill someone who's two blocks away, you'll have a hard time proving that it was in self-defense. At the same time, that powerful bullet can easily go through several walls, potentially killing the wrong person.

That's not to say that there's not a place for rifles in home defense. If you find yourself in a position where you are overwhelmed because your home is being attacked by an armed gang, then the only practical way to defend yourself is with rifles. Even so, those suitable for hunting aren't ideal for home defense. You'd be better off with some sort of AR-15, which is shorter, has a larger magazine capacity, and generally uses a smaller bullet.

While there are a lot of different rifle calibers, the best calibers to consider for home defense are .223/5.56mm and .308/7.62mm. These are the two calibers most used by the military and the most common ones for the AR-15. Being smaller, the .223/5.56mm is probably a better choice unless you're planning to use it for hunting as well.

Firearm Safety

While firearms are dangerous, treating them properly reduces the risk. Learn the four rules of firearm safety before even touching a gun. Make them your guide in how you use your firearms:

1. Always treat every firearm as if it's loaded, even if you've checked to see it is not.
2. Only point the firearm at things you are willing to destroy.
3. Always be sure of your target and what's behind it.
4. Only put your finger on the trigger or inside the trigger guard when you are ready to fire.

Defending yourself with a firearm isn't so much about the firearm you choose as it is about the shooter holding that firearm. Shooting is a skill, and it takes time and practice to learn how to do it well. Take the time to learn how to shoot properly by having someone teach you, and then practice at the shooting range. When you can get your shots into a 4-inch circle from 20 feet away with a pistol, you're on the right path.

While the consequent fight-or-flight reaction might help in a fistfight, it does the opposite for your shooting ability by reducing your fine motor skills by as much as 80%. If you can shoot that 4-inch circle on the range, you'll probably shoot one that's 5 times larger when facing off against someone shooting back at you. In other words, you'll miss more than you'll hit, which is why practice is so important.

Chapter 27
EDUCATE

Training is a key part of prepping and survival. While having the right tools and supplies is an important part of surviving any crisis, training is every bit as important. You can have the best gear and supplies there are, but if you don't know what to do with them, you'll die. On the other hand, with enough training, you will be able to get by without some of the "necessary" gear and supplies because you'll be prepared to find what you need and make your own gear.

Start learning survival skills now, but don't just learn them for yourself - teach them to your kids as well. If they're old enough to set the table for dinner, they're old enough to learn how to lay and start a fire.

The key with your kids is keeping them from telling all their friends and classmates what they're doing. Avoid using the words "prepper" and "prepping" around them. Rather, say that you're learning how to be ready for challenges when they come. You can even invoke the well-known Boy Scout motto, "Be Prepared." When the British soldier who came up with the idea of the Scouts was asked, "Be prepared for what?" He answered, "Well, anything." And that's what you're doing.

Avoid conspiracy theories and everything that comes across the news saying that the world is going to end. Speak with confidence about your life, and avoid focusing on any one TEOTWAWKI event. I've seen families who run drills about what to do in the event of a nuclear war or chemical warfare, as those are extreme situations that aren't likely to happen. It's better to focus on the problems that are more likely to impact your lives, like natural disasters.

Your attitude will be reflected by your children. Our children don't necessarily listen to everything we say, but they do tend to see everything we do. If you're going about your life always fearful that something is going to go wrong, you'll raise fearful kids. On the other hand, if you walk through life confident that you can meet any challenge that comes your way, they'll learn to be the same.

You can teach a lot of survival skills to your kids by taking them camping. Not only is that great family time, but if you tent camp rather than using a camper trailer, you're going to need to do things like light a fire, cut wood, and even purify water. They'll be learning survival skills just by learning camping skills. At the same time, you'll be leaving "prepping" out of it, so they won't go around telling their friends that they spent the weekend learning survival skills.

Shooting, whether guns or archery, are fun skills for your kids to learn. These skills don't have to be taught from a survival viewpoint. You can start teaching them to shoot with a pellet gun at 5 or 6 and with a .22 at 7 or 8. Of course, only do this if you feel your kids are responsible enough at that age, and never leave them unsupervised.

Working Through Survival Scenarios

Your kids might already know more than you think. Ask them. Maybe they've learned something in school, overheard you talking, or seen something in a movie. While Hollywood is great at exaggerating things, they do sometimes get it right.

You'll want to talk to your kids about what to do in the event of various survival scenarios. How will they get home if they have to? When should they leave school and head home, even if you don't call and tell them to? What do they do if a hurricane or tornado comes? What should they be doing to protect themselves if you haven't gotten home yet?

Stick to things that are likely to happen in the area where you live. If you live in Michigan, you're not likely to have a hurricane to worry about, but you *are* likely to deal with winter storms and power outages. Focus on that, especially at times when you're likely to experience it or when you just did.

One of the most useful things I've found is to do an after-action analysis of every disaster I hear about. I'll look at the available information, trying to find out what people experienced and what went wrong. From that, I look to see what lessons I can apply to my own preps. I did this when Hurricane Harvey flooded Houston. The Cajun Navy was there, rescuing people in their swamp boats, which made me realize that even though I don't live in a hurricane zone myself, flooding can happen anywhere. I needed something I could use to self-rescue if it flooded in my area. That "something" ended up being a low-cost option - a rubber raft.

Conclusion

If we lived in an ideal world, you'd never have to worry about protecting your home. But we don't live in such a world - if we did, we wouldn't have any need to be preppers. Previous disasters throughout the years have shown how desperate people can get and how far they will go to get what they think they need. If you're not prepared to deal with those people, you could suffer a much worse disaster.

That's not to say that we should be looking with anticipation toward the world falling apart so badly that it feels like we're living in the midst of *The Walking Dead*. You're much better off maintaining a low profile and avoiding getting involved in a fight. There are preppers who seem as though they're looking forward to lawlessness and a time when they can "prove themselves" through fighting.

The real danger is that the non-prepping community sees preppers as targets because of what they have, which could potentially lead to larger and larger attacks until preppers are ultimately overrun. Just because you succeed in fighting off one attack doesn't mean people will leave you alone.

System #8 - MASH: Medical, Accessories, Self-Defense, Hygiene

You never know when and where an emergency will happen

"By failing to prepare, you are preparing to fail."

— Benjamin Franklin

There are times when normal survival priorities don't matter. One of those is when you come under attack, as we discussed in the last system. Another is when a family member is injured. Chances are high that, at some point, someone will need some type of medical attention or first aid to survive.

Unfortunately, hospitals and clinics tend to become overrun during times of crisis, making it hard to get proper medical attention - assuming that you can even get to the hospital. If power is out and there's no fuel, you might have to walk there, pulling your injured family member in a cart. Once you get there, the hospital may or may not have the supplies necessary to provide treatment.

As a society, we've become dependent on others to take care of our medical needs. This is fine as long as everything is running smoothly, but in a time of emergency, it's important to be a bit more self-sufficient. In regard to injuries and illness, this means having the ability to administer first aid and cure (or at least ease the symptoms of) common illnesses.

Emergencies can happen at any time - while driving to church, hiking with the family, or even cooking dinner at home. Being prepared means being prepared *at all times*, as emergencies tend to pop up when you least expect them.

Chapter 28
Medical

When it comes to medical care from a survival standpoint, wound care is the most important aspect, as injuries are extremely likely to occur at some point during your survival journey.

Basic wound care consists of cleaning out the wound, stopping the bleeding, and keeping the wound clean and free of infection. Most of the items in a first-aid kit are used for this particular job. The basic process of wound treatment is as follows:

- Evaluate the patient (they may have more than one wound).
- Cut away clothing if necessary.
- Irrigate the wound to remove debris - use tweezers if necessary.

- Clean the wound with alcohol or hydrogen peroxide.
- Apply antiseptic ointment.
- Close the wound with butterfly closures or steri-strips if necessary.
- Bandage the wound and apply pressure to stop bleeding.
- Treat for shock (keep warm, legs raised).
- Transport for further medical treatment if necessary.

Other medical skills that you should consider learning include:

- CPR
- Treating choking
- Treating gunshot wounds (if you live in an area with a lot of hunters, hospitals may offer training classes for this)
- Applying a tourniquet [1]
- Making a splint
- Treating hypothermia
- Treating shock

First Aid

First aid is any immediate assistance given to someone with either a minor or serious injury or illness. The purpose of this care is to preserve life, prevent whatever condition is afflicting them from getting worse, and promote recovery.

Most commonly, first aid deals with stopping blood flow and helping to prevent infection from injury.

Anyone can administer first aid - it doesn't take a lot of training. However, getting trained is worth the time and effort. Taking care of an ax or bullet wound is much different than putting a bandage on a child's skinned knee. Some injuries are serious enough that proper first aid, not the hospital emergency room, is what saves the patient's life.

Survival can be dangerous, especially when you consider that you'll be performing jobs you've never done before, such as working with chainsaws and axes. The injuries that they can cause require a higher level of medical treatment than the average person can give.

Regardless of your skills today, it's time to bulk up on your knowledge and the first-aid supplies you have on hand. Most first-aid kits contain the bare minimum for handling minor cuts and scrapes. While that is valuable, it's not enough. Consider getting your hands on a trauma kit, whether you buy one or make your own.

To get started, pick up these basic first-aid supplies at the grocery store or pharmacy:

- Benadryl or antihistamine
- Calamine lotion or cortisone cream for itching
- Antiseptic cream or wipes - to kill bacteria and prevent infection

- Ibuprofen or other pain killers
- Bandages of various types
- Medical tape - duct tape and/or masking tape work in an emergency
- Rubbing alcohol and/or hydrogen peroxide - for cleaning wounds
- Medicines needed to treat chronic conditions that family members have - insulin, inhalers, antihypertensives, etc.

These items will give you a great first-aid starting point.

No matter what you do, you're going to need some references to work with, even after getting some training. *Where There is No Doctor* is my recommendation - it is the most widely read (and used) medical manual in the world, used by missionaries, peace corps volunteers, and preppers. *Where There is No Dentist* is the companion book for dealing with dental problems.

The FAK and the IFAK

The term IFAK was developed by the US Army and stands for "individual first-aid kit." Each soldier in a combat zone carries this so that the basics to treat a wound are always on hand. While not enough for everything, the idea is that the injured soldier's buddies can provide initial first-aid treatment before the medic arrives. It also ensures that each soldier has a bandage, so the medics don't have to carry around hundreds of them.

A FAK is simply a larger first-aid kit and can be referred to as a family first-aid kit. Not only does it have more than what each individual might carry, but it also provides multiples of each thing so that each kit can take care of multiple injuries. Any first-aid kit that only has one of each item should be backed up by a box of replacements and someone who will make sure that those replacements make it into the kit after each use.

A typical IFAK will consist of:

- Tourniquet
- Wound-packing gauze
- Pressure dressing and bandages
- Medical shears
- Nitrile gloves
- Rescue blanket

Again, it just contains the basics - its intent is to give the absolute necessities for taking care of a wounded soldier, assuming that a medical corpsman will be along in a minute and that they'll be carrying additional supplies. In the case of a bug out, it's a good idea to make sure that every family member has some sort of IFAK to make sure that there are enough first-aid supplies to go around.

For the larger FAK, there are many more items to obtain:[2]

- Tourniquet - the CAT tourniquet is the best
- Pressure dressing or Israeli bandage
- Gauze - either Z-fold, 4" squares, or rolls
- Cohesive medical tape and regular medical tape
- Medical shears
- Pain relievers, such as ibuprofen and acetaminophen
- Benadryl or other antihistamine
- Loperamide or Imodium for diarrhea
- Various types and sizes of adhesive bandages - cloth ones are recommended because of their flexibility
- Chest seal - in case of a chest wound from a bullet or knife
- Tweezers
- Irrigation syringe - for cleaning debris out of a wound
- Butterfly closures or steri-strips - to draw the skin back together on open cuts
- Aluminum splint - for broken bones
- Elastic bandages - for use with the aluminum splint
- Nitrile gloves
- Saline eye drops
- Nasopharyngeal airway - training is needed for this
- Emergency blankets
- Pepto-Bismol
- Antibiotics

- Arnica cream - Swiss Army knife of ointments for bruises, muscle aches, insect bites, etc.

This is actually a short list, and you may want to add to it as time goes on. Nevertheless, it's a good starting point for handling a variety of different situations. Specifically, it contains the basics to take care of the top four problems that preppers are likely to encounter:

- Wound care
- Pain and fever
- Upper respiratory infections
- Diarrhea

When Medicines Run Out

Long before the modern pharmaceutical industry came into existence, medicine existed. Back then, however, most medicine was either homeopathic or herbal. Today, major corporations produce artificial copies of the active ingredients in those natural remedies and sell them as medicine.

Should a TEOTWAWKI or other long-term survival situation arise, the only medicine that will likely be available will be homeopathic or herbal. Fortunately, there's a lot of information available on these remedies, but it will need to be downloaded and printed out now, before the disaster strikes.

Herbal medicine can be limited because not all herbs will grow in all areas. You can choose herbs that will grow in your area and add those to your garden. There are alternatives for most, so seek out substitutions for plants that won't grow in your area and plant those instead.

If you have family members who need prescription medicines for chronic conditions, stock up on their medications, especially if their dosage is stable. You'll need your physician's help if the medications require a prescription. It's a good idea to look for herbal remedies for those chronic conditions as an alternative if prescription medications run out.

Herbal medicine is an area that has been studied extensively; however, unlike over-the-counter medicines, you can't pick up an herb and read the label to see what it's useful for. Nor can you look up an ailment and find a cut-and-dried solution. What you'll find instead is a list of herbs that have properties that are useful for that condition.

A few common herbal treatments are:[3]

- Turmeric - pain and inflammation
- Peppermint - headache
- Ginger - nausea or upset stomach
- Chili peppers and coconut oil made into a cream - sore muscles
- Lavender - anxiety
- Any kind of mint - digestion

- Honey in tea - sore throat
- Echinacea - cold symptoms
- Elderberry - flu and virus
- Tea tree oil - fungus and bacteria

There are several ways to use the herbs as treatments for illness or injury. One option is to make a tea out of several different things that have been known to treat a particular condition.

Another good way to use these herbal remedies is with essential oils. Similar to the way that baking extracts take the flavor out of different foods and spices using alcohol, essential oils extract the healing nutrients from plants using oil. This puts the ingredients into an easy-to-store, compact form that's simple to administer.[4]

You can also purchase homeopathy kits, which contain small amounts of natural substances, such as minerals or plants. These kits generally come with a guide, which is an excellent starting point for homeopathy beginners. My own family uses one of these kits.

Chapter 29
Accessories

As you advance in your journey of stockpiling supplies and accumulating skills, there are additional tools and accessories that will be helpful.

You're Going to Need Tools

In modern society, we tend to think in terms of power tools, which makes sense if you want the easiest way to get the job done. However, those power tools may not work in a time of crisis, especially if the power is out. You're going to need hand tools to do everything from home repair, to gardening, to cutting wood. Now is the time to start collecting those tools and learning how to use them effectively.

That doesn't mean you should run out to Lowe's or Home Depot and fill a cart with tools - that gets very expensive very fast. Rather, you want to start thinking about the tools you'd like to have, and then gradually build up a collection. Garage and estate sales are great places to start, as they'll save you quite a bit of money versus buying new.

Beyond the basics like hammers, screwdrivers, and pliers, here are a few options to consider:

Tools for the shop:

- Bow saw or bucking saw - for cutting logs to length
- Ax and maul - for cutting down trees and splitting logs
- Scythe - for cutting the grass when the lawnmower won't
- Machete - useful for all sorts of garden cutting
- Spade - the basic digging shovel
- Posthole digger - useful for more than building fences
- Hand drill
- Hand saws of various types
- Sharpening stones

Tools for the kitchen:

- Manual can opener
- Hand-crank grain mill
- Tea kettle - cast iron will allow you to use it over the fire or on the barbecue grill

- Coffee percolator
- Canning equipment
- Solar dehydrator - can also be used as a solar oven
- Wood cookstove - rather expensive, but it will work when the power is out

Stock Sanitation Supplies

COVID demonstrated the need to stockpile sanitation supplies. Toilet paper wasn't the only thing that flew off the shelves at the beginning of the pandemic. Hand sanitizer, cleaning supplies, bleach, and personal hygiene supplies sold out too. You'll want to stock:

- Toilet paper (lots of toilet paper)
- Antibacterial cleaning wipes
- Hand sanitizer
- Soap and shampoo
- Baby wipes (also useful for adults)
- Toothbrushes, toothpaste, and dental floss
- Deodorant
- Feminine hygiene supplies
- Basic home cleaning supplies, including disinfectants
- Laundry detergent
- Dish soap
- Garbage bags and zip-top bags in various sizes

There are reusable cloth options for diapers, feminine hygiene, and even toilet paper; however, cleaning those cloth supplies can be tricky. While it is possible, it means having the soap and water to clean them with.

Other Needs

You may have family members with some additional health needs, like glasses or contacts. If anyone wears glasses, you'll want to always have at least one spare pair on hand for them. This can be the last pair of glasses that you save when they get a new prescription. In addition, make sure you have cleaning supplies for those glasses.

People who use contact lenses will have a bigger problem, as contact lenses are disposable. You could buy a year's worth of contacts and keep them on hand along with the necessary cleaning solution, but you'll also want to have glasses available because you may eventually run out of contacts.

If you have babies or elderly family members, they're likely to have certain needs as well. Don't just think about what they need today - think a year or two down the road. If grandma is likely to need a walker soon, it's best to buy it now and add it to your prepping stocks, even if that means buying a used one. Babies have a lot of needs as well, and they're constantly changing.

Consider buying your kids' clothing two years ahead. Don't just buy the clothes that they need for this year, buy the clothes that they'll need in two years, and then box them up according to size. As they grow, you'll be pulling their clothes out of the attic or basement, then adding another year's stock for two years away. By stocking up ahead of time, you'll always have a couple of years' worth of different-sized clothing available in case of emergency.

Chapter 30
Self-Defense

In 2020, a terrifying home invasion took place in the Omaha home of UFC light-heavyweight contender Anthony "Lionheart" Smith. While Anthony, his wife, mother-in-law, and three daughters were asleep, a break-in occurred. Smith was able to subdue the unarmed, screaming intruder after a 5-minute altercation that involved what he described as a violent wrestling match where he was eventually able to pin the assailant down before the police arrived. Fortunately, no one in the Smith family was injured, only shaken up by what took place that morning.

It's not clear why this man broke in and started screaming at the top of his lungs. Anthony Smith, one of the baddest dudes on planet Earth, called it "one of the toughest fights" he has ever had with this 170-pound average Joe. Smith weighs 240 pounds and is currently ranked as the #7 contender in his division. The takeaway is that even a professional fighter with a plan can struggle with a single person breaking in unexpectedly.

Smith went on to say that, admittedly, he got sloppy, and, in hindsight, that left his family exposed. He lives in a safe neighborhood where it's easy to "forget" to lock your car doors, set the alarm, or even close the garage door. He had failed to do all three of those things that evening. He also mentioned that the gun he typically keeps in his nightstand was left in a bag away from his reach.

There are many types of self-defenses out there - some use words, some use your physical strength, and some use weapons. Smith may have made some mistakes as far as his home defenses, but he was able to use his knowledge of self-defense to handle this invasion before it got ugly.

Violence as a Last Resort

It's a general principle of the law in the United States that you can use deadly force for self-defense. The application of this principle varies from state to state, but, regardless of where you live, if it comes down to using deadly force to protect your loved ones, you'll need to be able to prove that you acted in self-defense.

Even if you see several armed men coming down the street, and you're convinced that they're heading for your home, you can't shoot at them. It's not self-defense until they either shoot at you or make it clear that they are going to, which probably won't happen until they're on your property.

If you do find yourself in a situation similar to the one above, the best way to start is by talking to the threat first. By using your emotional intelligence, oftentimes you can diffuse a situation before it escalates.

Start by assessing the threat. Is it one person or a group? Do they have weapons? Do you? Are you backed up against a wall so that they have your exit point covered? There are many things to work out while your adrenaline is pumping, but if you remain calm and try to keep talking things out, this buys you valuable time. You have the option of locating your weapon, moving closer toward an exit to escape, or assessing the assailant's purposes further.

After evaluating the situation, there are a few tactics to try before resorting to violence:

- **Avoid** - Keep a low profile, don't pick fights, and don't brag to anyone about your stockpile. If people don't know who you are or what you have, they're less likely to come looking for you when they need supplies.
- **Engage in a conversation** - If a confrontation happens, be friendly and attempt to communicate clearly. Ask questions that could distract or make your opponent realize that neither of you wants a

fight today.

- **Introduce yourself by name** - Ask the other person for his name as well. This makes it personal and is a great way to get history quick - maybe you'll even bond with him.
- **Peace offering** - Maybe you have a bottle of vodka or an extra loaf of bread that can be offered up in exchange for leaving you alone.
- **Run or Hide** - In certain circumstances, like we often tell children, it's best to run and hide. It's that simple.
- **Toss-and-run approach** - In keeping with the running away theme, let's use a supply backpack as an example. If the other person is threatening you, don't simply hand the backpack over - toss it in his direction, move quickly backward, and get out of there as quickly as possible.

Some of these ideas may be the opposite of what you'd like to do, but they may also be just the thing to help you avoid a scrum or a potentially fatal encounter. Think of your family. Is it best for them if you escalate this situation into violent chaos? Probably not.

Hopefully you can find peace in the fact that you did attempt to engage in an honorable way before resorting to violence. Sometimes, though, there are occasions when talking and being nice simply isn't effective, and you'll have no choice but to defend yourself or your family.

Plus, at this point, there is now a very high probability that whatever you're about to do can be classified as self-defense in the eyes of the law.

Improving Your Self-Defense Skills

There are a variety of classes that you can take to improve self-defense skills. See if you can find any of these in your area:

- **Brazilian jiu-jitsu (BJJ)** - This is a grappling and ground fighting martial art that has seen massive growth in the last decade. BJJ focuses on non-violent submission of your opponent using takedowns and other holds. It's also an excellent workout.
- **Marksmanship class** - Practice makes perfect. The more range time you can get to practice your shot with an instructor present, the better you'll be under pressure. This is not limited to firearms - consider archery as well.
- **Hand-to-hand combat training** - This could include training with mace or pepper spray, knives, or simple street fighting and more. Start by signing up for a personal security training class - Fieldcrest Survival & Sheepdog Response are great places to start your research.

While it's best to avoid an altercation altogether, sometimes that just isn't a possibility. There may come a time when you'll need to fight to defend your home or your family.

Chapter 31
Hygiene

Personal hygiene is an important part of maintaining health. We don't normally think of it that way because we are so far removed from the basics of survival. But without good personal hygiene, we are much more susceptible to disease, as well as a number of skin conditions, infections, and dental problems. The social part of not smelling bad is just a bonus.

Maintaining personal hygiene when water is at a premium is challenging. Having one gallon of water per person per day doesn't include enough water for bathing or washing clothes. Yet we need to do these things if we are going to avoid disease. Hygiene becomes especially important if an epidemic breaks out, which can certainly happen in the event that water and sewer services are lost, making it so that people can't maintain their personal hygiene.

Keeping Clean

To start with, it is possible to bathe with one-half to one gallon of water, as they do in many third-world countries. All that's needed is a bucket and a small plastic container. Put a gallon or so of water in the bucket and head for the shower. Place shampoo in your hair, spreading it out as much as possible. Use the plastic container to scoop out a few cups of water, pouring it over your head to wet your hair. Lather, then work your way down your body, using the residual water on your body and soap to wash. The remainder of the water is used sparingly to rinse your body and hair, starting from the top and working your way down.

Placing dirty clothing in the bottom of the shower and stopping up the drain allows you to wash the clothing at the same time, walking on the clothing to work your shampoo and soap into the clothing. It's not a perfect solution, but it's better than nothing.

As we learned during COVID, we can keep our hands clean with hand sanitizer, as the concern is eliminating bacteria and viruses. Hand sanitizer can also help to get the worst of the dirt off your hands at the same time, assuming you wipe your hands on a towel instead of just rubbing them until the sanitizer dries.

Dealing with Human Waste

One of the greatest medical discoveries in history has been the fact that human waste spreads disease. Human waste is one of the dirtiest substances on the planet, biologically speaking. It contains millions of bacteria which can cause and spread disease.

Our modern sanitary sewer system protects us from illness and disease by collecting and purifying wastewater from our sinks and toilets. But we may very well not have the sewer system available to us if the power and water are out. We'll need to deal with our bodily fluids (and solids) in other ways. There are four basic options:

- **Septic tank** – If your home has a septic tank, that should take care of your waste for a couple of years.
- **Outhouse** – The old-fashioned way of dealing with human waste is to dig an outhouse, keeping it far enough away from the home to avoid the stench. Adding ashes from the fire or lye to the pit can help keep the smell down.
- **Pail Toilet** – If you don't have an outhouse and can't dig one, then a pail toilet will allow you to collect human waste in plastic bags, saving it for a time when the crisis is over and it can be taken to the sewage treatment plant for disposal.
- **Humanure Composting** – Human waste can be composted, allowing you to use it as nutrients for

your garden. Special composting toilets exist for this purpose, or you can simply take the waste and add it to your compost bin along with the green matter.

Conclusion

Health, hygiene, first aid, and self-defense are easy areas to overlook in the push to prepare for a disaster, but they are just as important as having enough food to eat. It will do your family no good to have a year's worth of food stocked up if your family is attacked and robbed or if everyone falls victim to an epidemic and dies.

While the grocery stores emptied out of just about everything during the global pandemic in 2020, it was cleaning supplies and personal hygiene supplies that were cleaned out first and were some of the last items to be restocked. People were desperate for PPE (personal protection equipment), cleaning supplies, masks, and hand sanitizer for a long time. We must be ready for the next one.

The average person has very little in the way of medical knowledge or self-defense skills. We depend on doctors, nurses, and law enforcement to keep us healthy and alive. However, with the vast amount of information that is available on the internet, we can all gain competence in first aid and self-defense, even if we don't become experts.

System #9 - STOP: Stop, Think, Observe, Plan

Bugging Out for Survival

"One of these days the clocks will stop, and time won't mean a thing. One of these days their bombs will drop and silence everything. But it's alright, yeah it's alright, I said it's alright."

— Dave Grohl/Foo Fighters, "One of These Days"

In most situations, it makes sense to bug in and stay home, rather than bugging out. Even so, there are times when that is impossible. At the time of this writing, Hurricane Ian is crossing the Florida peninsula, bringing storm surge flooding of over 12 feet and washing away houses. Anyone who decided to bug in for that hurricane was in trouble.

Hurricanes aren't the only situation when bugging out is required. In 2018, the Camp Fire swept through the town of Paradise, California, burning all 1,200 buildings to the ground. No matter how well-prepared you are, there is no way to survive bugging in for an event like that. Even staying in an underground shelter would be ill-advised, as the fire would consume all the oxygen.

Scenarios like these may not be common, but they do exist, so we all need to have a bug-out plan. If your home becomes untenable, you've got to be ready to evacuate quickly, which means being packed, knowing where you're going, and knowing how you're going to get there.

Chapter 32
STOP

If your family is forced to leave your home in the case of an emergency event, stop what you're doing, remain calm, and analyze the situation. Take a few deep breaths. What has happened is in the past, and you can't change it. To stay alive and move forward, you will need to make rational decisions, which is best done when you're calm and have a clear mind. Hopefully there is already an evacuation plan in place, as well as a backup plan or two.

People bug out for different reasons, at different times, and with different goals. Some bug out temporarily to avoid a disaster, and others plan on leaving home forever. Circumstances dictate a lot of this, but much depends on the individual and what they're hoping to accomplish.

You may never know in advance exactly when or why you might need to bug out. For that reason, you should have at least two different bug out plans with different destinations, plus you can always mix and match between the two, if needed.

The first plan is an emergency evacuation (EE – escape and evasion). This is what is done to avoid a natural disaster or pending attack that could overwhelm your home. An emergency evacuation is intended to be short-term, with the idea of returning home sometime in the future. This differs greatly from a planned evacuation (INCH – I'm Never Coming Home) - something you would only want to do if your home was about to be destroyed or in the case of societal collapse, where it would be safer to get away from everyone.

While these two might seem very similar, there are some huge differences between them. In the case of an EE, your bug-out bag only needs to get you to a planned place of safety where you'll have the supplies you need in order to survive. For most, that means only 3 to 5 days of supplies. But in the case of an INCH, your bug-out bag isn't so much about having the short-term supplies as it is about having long-term survival gear.

Bugging In vs. Bugging Out

One of the biggest questions that any prepper must face is *where* they're going to survive. Granted, there are some situations that don't give us that option, like driving off the road in the midst of a blizzard. For most disasters, though, we have enough time to bug out before disaster strikes.

The term "bug out" comes from the military. During the early days of the Korean War, there were many units suffering from "bug-out fever," abandoning their posts and retreating because they were so badly outnumbered by the North Koreans. It has since become a term used for leaving a location that is no longer tenable, especially in the prepping and survival community.

Bugging *in* makes more sense than bugging *out* for most people, because most of us aren't really prepared to go out in the woods and live off the land. Staying in your home provides you with shelter, even if your home becomes damaged. You also have access to your stockpile, as well as everything else you own, much of which may be useful or make you comfortable in surviving.

Even so, everyone needs a bug-out plan, as it's impossible to know if or when you might be forced to bug out. The people living in Southeast Houston weren't expecting Hurricane Harvey to dump over 3 feet of rain on their city, flooding their homes. Even those who were prepared had to bug out because their homes were no longer livable - at least for the short-term.

Or, how about the people living in the town of Paradise, California, in 2018? Their entire town, all 1,200 buildings, were burnt to the ground by the Camp Fire. Everyone had to evacuate, or they would have died.

Some people use the term "shelter in place" instead of bugging in, but that's a misuse of the term. Shelter in place is a technical term used by government agencies when it is necessary to stay indoors in order to avoid a chemical or natural gas leak. The idea is to stay indoors with the doors and windows closed, wherever you are, so that you don't breathe the chemicals in.

The Bug-Out Bag

A bug-out bag is nothing more than a pre-packed kit that contains everything you'll need to get from your home to your survival shelter. So, in reality, you've got to have an idea of where you're going before preparing your bug-out bag. Otherwise, you're going to be carrying things you won't need and forgetting things you do need.

Most bug-out bags are built in a backpack. While it's not a requirement, a backpack is easier to carry if you must abandon your vehicle and go on foot. Avoid tactical back-packs, as they are a bit too obvious; rather, pick a good back-packing model. It will be lighter and have more space inside.

Any bug-out bag must meet your basic survival needs of maintaining your body heat and having clean drinking water and food to eat. Please note any bug-out bag needs to be customized based on your own needs and survival skills. Here's a list of what to include:

- Backpack
- Backpacking sleeping bag (attached outside)
- Mattress pad (attached outside)
- Emergency food - 3 to 5 days of MREs or freeze-dried backpacking food, energy bars, high-energy snacks
- P-38 can opener - in case you find canned food
- Lifestraw or other water purifying system
- Backpacking cook kit, utensils, spices
- Canteen or water bottle, preferably filled - use a metal one, so that it can be put in the fire to purify water if necessary
- Backpacking stove - avoid propane and choose wood burning instead
- At least two types of reliable fire starters that will work in wet weather
- Fire accelerant, such as WetFire cubes or cotton balls coated in petroleum jelly
- Individual first-aid kit (IFAK)
- Mylar survival blanket - the heavy-duty kind, not the disposable ones
- Backpacking tent or ultralight tarp for making a tent

- Paracord - 100 feet minimum
- Duct tape
- Change of rugged clothing, plus extra socks and underwear
- Rain poncho
- Headlamp with rechargeable batteries
- Solar battery charger
- Wallet with ID and credit card, plus laminated list of phone numbers
- Multitool
- Waterproof paper and pencil, sharpie
- USB with copies of all your important documents
- Machete (strapped to outside)
- Pistol and rifle, along with spare ammo
- Camp hatchet, preferably with hammer back for driving tent stakes
- Folding shovel
- Folding pruning saw - best camp/survival saw there is
- Spare contacts and solution if you wear them, extra eyeglasses in a case
- Personal hygiene kit - soap, toothbrush, dental floss, deodorant, tweezers, razor, etc.
- Dude wipes
- Toilet paper
- Antibacterial hand cleaner
- Hand-crank radio for news
- Walkie-talkies for every member of your group

- Water resistant dry bag (store clothes inside)

The INCH Bag

An INCH bag will be much like the bug-out bag, with a few notable differences. First, you don't want to concern yourself so much with consumable items, such as matches, food, and batteries. Stick with replenishable items, such as:

- Ferro rod or metal match for starting fire, rather than wood matches
- Fishing gear, lightweight traps or snares, and seed, rather than food
- Solar charger or hand-crank charger, rather than batteries
- Recurve bow, rather than a rifle (you can make arrows for a recurve bow, but not for a compound bow)

Keep in mind that your maximum pack weight should be no more than 20% of your body weight. If you're overweight or out of shape, you'll need to cut that some, as you won't be able to comfortably carry 20% of your body weight all day.

Your Bug-Out Vehicle

You don't need a fancy bug-out vehicle like those that people love to show on social media. You most likely won't even need 4-wheel-drive. Rather, you need a reliable, inconspic-uous vehicle that can carry you from your home to your survival retreat. It should have enough range to drive the necessary distance, enough room for your family, and enough cargo space for everyone's bug-out bags.

The most important part of your bug-out vehicle is reliabil-ity. Keep it maintained, with good tires, preventative mainte-nance completed regularly, and plenty of fuel on hand. A few full gas cans can save you from having to wait in line at the gas stations when everyone else is there. Besides, gas stations tend to run out of gas during an evacuation.

Keep some emergency equipment in the vehicle as well, including emergency survival equipment and the tools and supplies needed to take care of vehicle emergencies.

Bugging out should never be anyone's "Plan A" unless they truly do have that proverbial cabin in the woods that's ready to be used as a survival retreat. For the rest of us, the best plan is to stay at home unless we're forced to evacuate by our circumstances. Evacuations are unpredictable, so a solid bug-out plan is needed, which should include having a place to go, knowing what to bring, and having a plan to get there.

Ideally, you want more than one bug-out plan. Not all disas-ters are the same, so they aren't all going to require the same evacuation plan. There's always a chance that Plan A isn't going to work - for example, if the natural disaster that's hitting you is also hitting your primary survival retreat.

Be sure to practice your bug out a few times, getting the whole family involved. This is an excellent way to verify your plan as well as train your family. Expect to find issues during the first run-through or two - that's normal. Each time will get better, and eventually you'll have a plan that you know will work.

Chapter 33
THINK

The key to any successful bug out is planning. When the time comes to leave your home, you're not going to have time to think about what you need, where you're going, or how you're going to get there - all of this needs to be decided ahead of time. It's much easier to plan your bug out when you can think calmly, rather than trying to figure it all out during a crisis.

The first question to ask is where you're going, as everything hinges on that. This should be a location that's far enough away that it won't be dealing with the same disaster, while still being close enough that you can get there without having to stop for gas. There are lots of possibilities, such as:

- An alternate property you own, such as a vacation place or cabin in the woods

- The home of a friend or family member out in the country
- A campground
- A rural town where you're known
- A hotel where you know the owners and can get them to hold a room
- FEMA or Red Cross emergency evacuation shelter (not recommended)

Regardless of the destination, you want to visit the location and make sure that it will work for you. A horde of other people may be bugging out at the same time. How will you ensure that you have a place to stay? What can you do to guarantee it?

Once you've found a place, it's a good idea to establish a supply cache there. Renting a small storage unit is ideal for this. This will ensure that you have supplies, while also planting your flag in that location. If a rural town, for example, is trying to keep strangers out, but you can prove that you have supplies stored there, then you have a claim to enter the town. It's even better if you know a few people in the town.

With a destination in mind, it's time to consider the route to get there. Avoid major highways and intersections as much as possible. Plan on taking secondary highways and county roads to avoid traffic. Drive the route and make sure you know it well.

Don't stop there though - you'll want to select alternative routes you can use, as well as crossovers to get from one route to the other. What if you have to set out on foot or abandon your vehicle? How will that affect your route?

Make sure you have both road maps and topographical maps for your entire route, including alternates. It takes some time to get used to topographical maps, but they can give you a lot of useful information, like where to find water. Get a good compass and learn how to use it, and practice locating your-self on the topographical map by shooting bearings to obvious landmarks. If you get lost or have to change your route, perhaps going cross-country on foot, that skill will be invaluable.

Setting Up Camp

It is likely that you'll have to spend at least a few nights out in the open during your bug out or at your survival retreat. Camping out can be an enjoyable time, even in these sorts of circumstances. But it's a good idea to stop at least two hours before sunset to give yourself time to set up camp before it gets dark.

If you don't have a watch or don't know what time sunset is, you can use your hand to find out. Stretch your arm out, with your hand horizontal and the pinkie on the horizon. Measure how many finger-widths the sun is above the hori-zon, using both hands if necessary. Each finger is about 15 minutes, so you should be stopping when you're eight fingers above the horizon.

You'll want to set up camp in a place that provides shelter from wind and rain and prevents people from seeing you. If you've been traveling along a road or trail, move off to the side where you won't be so obvious. Don't camp right by the water, as that invites both wild animals and others who are bugging out too. Stay at least 100 yards away, and then fill up your canteens and water bottles in the morning before heading out.

There are two main things that need to be done before the sun goes down - starting a fire and erecting a shelter. There should be a tarp or tent in your bug-out bag, which will make putting up a temporary shelter easy. However, you may still need to cut a ridge pole for your tent. You'll also need to cut enough wood for your fire to last the night.

Always make sure your fire is small and safely contained so it can't spread. A small campfire is less obvious to passersby - this isn't the time for a roaring campfire. You want something just big enough to warm your food over. If it's cold, make sure that you build a reflector behind it to heat your shelter.

A Dakota fire hole is an excellent option for your fire. This consists of a hole in the ground where your fire is built. Another smaller hole, angling from the bottom of the hole off to the side, provides a constant air supply that helps the fire burn. Since the fire is built in the hole, below ground level, it is less visible and there's less chance of it starting a forest fire.

Chapter 34
OBSERVE

Although living off the land is not normally recommended as a bug-out strategy, there may come a time when it is necessary. The main problem with trying to live off the land is that there are more people than there are wild game animals to hunt. That's especially true in the eastern half of the country, although some parts of the west are sparsely populated enough that it would be possible to live off of what can be caught by hunting and trapping.

Nevertheless, it's a good idea to be prepared to hunt, fish, trap, and forage for food. Even if you have a stockpile or cache of food at your survival retreat, it will have limits. Being able to add to that from the bounty of nature will help your stockpile go further. Should the situation turn into a long-term survival scenario, being able to harvest food from nature may be necessary to keep your family alive.

Hunting

When we talk about hunting, we tend to talk mostly about big game hunting. While hunting big game will provide a larger amount of meat when you get an animal, big game is far outnumbered by small game. You don't want to forget about hunting for rabbits, squirrels, and other small game.

The majority of hunting today consists of sitting in a raised blind and waiting for deer or other animals to come along and eat from feed corn that has been spread on the ground, but that's not likely what you'll be doing in a survival situation. Rather, you're going to have to rely on your knowledge of the animals you are hunting, picking a place to await your intended targets where they're likely to cross your path by finding their trails, watering holes, or grazing areas.

Animals depend on their sense of smell much and can easily detect the human scent. If they smell you, they'll hide or leave the area. The wind can be used to your advantage - stay downwind of where you expect to find the animals.

The best time to hunt is early in the morning. Most animals will wake and go to their favorite watering hole or grazing area. Finding game trails or watering holes is a boon, as it allows you to stake out those areas and await the arrival of your quarry.

Don't limit your thinking to hunting with a rifle. There are several silent weapons that are excellent for hunting, such as bows, crossbows, blowguns, slingshots, or spears.

Trapping

Small game and birds don't necessarily need to be hunted - they can be trapped. This can be achieved using either commercially made traps or do-it-yourself traps and snares.

One of the keys to successful trapping is finding an appropriate place to set the snares. The best location is a place where you know that the animals will be, which means looking for their feeding locations, finding their trails, or finding their burrows. The snare is then built where it's inevitable that they'll trip it while doing their normal activities. Using food to bait the traps and snares is very helpful too, especially for snares that are on the ground.

Rat traps make a good makeshift trap for squirrels. Another great way to trap squirrels is to make nooses out of snare wire or guitar strings and attach them to a fallen branch. Lean that branch against a tree with the loops from your nooses on the top side. Squirrels will run up that, rather than the tree trunk, hanging themselves in the process.

Fishing

Typically, there are more fish in the water than there are animals in the forest, and they tend to be easier to catch. Even so, survival fishing is usually different from sport fishing. You can't afford a whole day of lounging on the bank, casting your bait out into the water, and lazily reeling it back in. Rather, you need to use methods that allow you the greatest chance of catching fish with minimal effort, which may mean using some sort of trap, whether it is a net trap, or one made by pounding sticks into the stream bottom. Another good option is an automatic reel, which will pull in the line when the fish go for the bait on the hook. Attached to a tree or shrub, those automatic reels will hold your catch until you get there.

Foraging

A diet of meat alone is not sufficient; you'll need to augment your diet with plants. The challenge lies in picking the right plants to eat. Eating the wrong plants can be dangerous, as many plants (or parts of plants) are poisonous.

Buy a good guide with pictures to help you identify edible plants. Make sure that it covers the part of the country you live in. Not all guides are the same and it won't do you any good to have one for the northwest if you live in the east. Different plants grow in different parts of the country.

Take some time walking in the woods, seeking out these plants and getting familiar with them. It doesn't hurt to harvest some and try cooking them as well. Their flavor will likely be different than you expect, so you may need to practice a little in order to make them palatable.

Chapter 35
PLAN

For many preppers, the ideal survival retreat is to have a cabin in the woods somewhere. However, those cabins can be too expensive to make the idea feasible.

One option that can work out almost as good is to turn a recreational vehicle into a survival retreat. Recreational vehicles are designed to be lived in just about anywhere. All furniture and storage are provided in a compact, mobile package. With a few modifications, they can be used for long-term off-grid living.

There are two possibilities to consider. The first is to buy a piece of property and park the RV on it, turning it into a fixed survival retreat. The other option is to set up the RV as a mobile survival retreat and have a variety of places where you know you can park it - campgrounds, friends' properties, wide spots in the road, parking lots, or any combination thereof.

The key to making this a viable option is to have a way to resupply all the built-in infrastructure items that the RV normally provides for you:

- **Water** – You must have a water source, of course. Purified water can go in the RV's freshwater tank, allowing you to use it like normal. Avoid putting non-purified water in the tank to not contaminate the system. Adding a good filtration system is a good idea, which will allow you to use water that hasn't been purified.
- **Sewage** – The onboard gray and black water tanks will fill in a few days. You can buy a rolling tank that you can empty them into, which can then be carted off and dumped somewhere, such as a hole in the ground. If you're going to set up your RV on property you own, you can build a septic system out of a couple of 55-gallon plastic drums. Add some perforated plastic pipe for a leach field and you're ready to go.
- **Propane** – If things really go bad, you're not going to be able to resupply propane. Having an extra couple of tanks and a way to connect them to the RV's system will expand the time you'll have propane available. You'll still run out eventually, so avoid using it for anything you don't need.

- **Cooking** – Should be done over a campfire rather than using up propane.
- **Bathing** – Heat the water over the campfire and bathe out of a bucket to1 save both water and propane.
- **Electricity** – Unless you end up going to a campground, you're probably going to need to be able to generate your own electricity. Even if your RV has a generator, you'll probably have trouble finding fuel after the first few days. You may need wind or solar power.

How Many Solar Panels?

One challenge with going off-grid in a RV is generating electrical power. For most people, that means solar panels. Wind turbines are actually more efficient if you happen to be in an area where you have steady winds, but the best bet is to do both so that you have power whether without the sun or without the wind.

The RV's batteries are the limiting factor. A larger RV will typically have two deep-cycle batteries to provide power to the entire RV. If it is a motorhome, there will be a third battery for the engine, but the two systems will be isolated from each other except through a solenoid for emergency starts.

The deep-cycle batteries provide a reserve capacity of 360 minutes (180 minutes each), which converts to 150 Ah (amp-hours) of power. However, solar panels and wind turbines are rated in watts. What this means is that you need 900 watts of solar and/or wind charging capability to keep those batteries fully charged. The size and efficiency of the panels will determine how many are needed to provide power to the RV. Even with solar panels, though, it's important to be mindful about electrical usage so that you don't use more power than your system is generating.

Conclusion

Preparation is a requirement of prepping. Yes, that's redundant, but it's the truth! Hall of Fame football coach Vince Lombardi said it best: "Everyone has a will to win, but very few have the will to <u>prepare</u> to win."

Emergencies don't make appointments; you likely won't have an hour to go running all around the house, discussing your plan and trying to locate all the things your family will need in an already stressful situation. Your proper gear must be packed, your plan accounted for, and your team ready to go.

My strong recommendation is this: Buy duplicate kits for the sole purpose of bugging out. This could get expensive, and we're definitely trying to keep your budget in mind.

However, the alternative is that you'll waste crucial time discussing, planning, and gathering supplies once the chaos has started. There really is no price tag too high when it comes to the importance of stopping, thinking, observing, and planning for evacuation.

The Final Word

The beginning of your prepping journey can seem a bit overwhelming, especially after receiving so much information in such a short time. You probably feel like you've been drinking from a firehose. Don't worry - nobody is saying that you need to do everything today, this week, or even this year. Rather, I encourage you to pick an area and start. Almost everyone starts out small, adding to their preparedness bit by bit. You'll be surprised just how fast your family's security grows. Each step, no matter how small, makes your family more secure and increases their chances of survival.

Isn't that what it's all about? You've already taken the first step by buying and reading this book. You are doing something good for your family. Take heart in that, and be encouraged to get started on the road ahead. Remember how important a positive mental attitude is for survival, and start practicing it now.

Get your family involved. You might get some foot dragging and complaints, but you're ultimately doing it for them. Try to avoid making a chore out of prepping and make it fun, especially when learning survival skills. Kids will get on board faster than you think, especially when you're teaching them how to do cool stuff, like lighting a fire, that their friends don't know how to do.

You're about to embark on what could be the most exciting journey of your life. Take time to enjoy it. Learning is fun and learning how to do the things you need to know in order to survive can be especially fun. Allow yourself that pleasure, whether it is in planting your garden, learning first-aid, or working on survival skills while going camping.

Good luck on the journey.

As an independent author with a small marketing budget, reviews are my livelihood on this platform. I would be incredibly thankful if you could take just 60 seconds to write a brief review on Amazon, even if it's just a few sentences! You can do so by clicking the link below. I love hearing from my readers, and I personally read every single review.

Scan the QR code below!

Leave a 1-Click Review!

Customer reviews

★★★★★ 5 out of 5

170 global ratings   share your thoughts with other customers

5 star		100%
4 star		0%
3 star		0%
2 star		0%
1 star		0%

Write a review

HOW TO GET $49 WORTH OF PREPPER'S CONTENT

FREE

- Free bonus #1: Food Storage Family Inventory Calculator Spreadsheet   ($19 value)

- Free bonus #2: Walmart Shopping List ($12 value)

- Free bonus #3: Recipes Made From Your Prepper Pantry ($10 value)

- Free bonus #4: Bug Home Guide ($8 value)

All of this 100% FREE, with no strings attached! You don't need to enter any details except your email address.

To receive your bonuses scan the QR code below:

SCAN ME

Notes

7. Positive MENTAL Attitude

1. 98.6 Degrees, by Cody Lundin

10. Chapter 10 - DEVELOP Your Plan

1. https://www.redcross.org/about-us/news-and-events/news/Learn-More-about-Red-Cross-Safe-and-Well-App-Feature-and-Website.html

12. ANALYZE the Results

1. The Cajun Navy is a volunteer organization from Louisiana. They use their boats, many of which are swamp boats, to perform search-and-rescue operations, as well as provide disaster relief.

14. IT: It's All About the Food on Hand

1. https://theprepared.com/homestead/guides/supermarket-food-list/

28. Medical

1. https://www.wikihow.com/Apply-a-Tourniquet
2. https://theprepared.com/bug-out-bags/guides/first-aid-kit-list/
3. https://www.allinahealth.org/healthysetgo/heal/natural-remedies-for-everyday-illnesses
4. https://earth911.com/living-well-being/essential-oils-10-remedies/

References

Lundin. (2003b). *98.6 Degrees: The Art of Keeping Your Ass Alive: Lundin, Cody, Miller, Russ: 9781586852344: Amazon.com: Books*. https://www.amazon.com/98-6-Degrees-Keeping-Your-Alive/dp/1586852345

Let Family Know You're Safe - Use Red Cross App and Website. (2017). https://www.redcross.org/about-us/news-and-events/news/Learn-More-about-Red-Cross-Safe-and-Well-App-Feature-and-Website.html

Food list: How to build your survival pantry with long-lasting food from the supermarket. (2022, October 17). The Prepared. https://theprepared.com/homestead/guides/supermarket-food-list/

Poindexter, J. (2019, October 29). *Vegetable Garden Size Calculator: How Much to Plant for Your Family*. MorningChores. https://morningchores.com/vegetable-garden-size/

Live Ladybugs and other Beneficial Insects to control Pest Insects. (n.d.). NaturesGoodGuys. Retrieved 11 November 2022, from https://www.naturesgoodguys.com/

Litza, J. (2022, February 22). *How to Apply a Tourniquet: 9 Steps (with Pictures)*. wikiHow. https://www.wikihow.com/Apply-a-Tourniquet

Rader, T. (2022, August 1). *IFAK first aid kit list*. The Prepared. https://theprepared.com/bug-out-bags/guides/first-aid-kit-list/

Sloun, N. (2015, November 28). *Natural remedies for everyday illnesses*. https://www.allinahealth.org/healthysetgo/heal/natural-remedies-for-everyday-illnesses

www.ingramcontent.com/pod-product-compliance
Lightning Source LLC
Chambersburg PA
CBHW022046020426
42335CB00012B/571